Text
ANNAMARIA LILLA MARIOTTI

Project Editor
VALERIA MANFERTO DE FABIANIS

Editorial Coordination
NOVELLA MONTI

Graphic Designer
CLARA ZANOTTI

Editorial staff
ALBERTO BERTOLAZZI
MARIA VALERIA URBANI GRECCHI

© 2005 White Star S.p.a.
Via Candido Sassone, 22/24
13100 Vercelli, Italy
www.whitestar.it
TRANSLATION: Sarah Ponting

ISBN 88-544-0088-2

REPRINTS:
1 2 3 4 5 6   09 08 07 06 05
Printed in China
Color separation by Chiaroscuro, Turin

LIGHTHOUSES

LIGHTHOUSES

CONTENTS

INTRODUCTION

1 ■ Kéréon Lighthouse, Brittany (France).

2-3 ■ Pierres Noires Lighthouse, Brittany (France).

4 ■ Sambro Island Lighthouse, Nova Scotia (Canada).

5 ■ Le Four Lighthouse, Brittany (France).

6 left ■ La Jument Lighthouse, Brittany (France).

6 right ■ Lighthouse during a storm on the Atlantic coast.

7 ■ Point Reyes Lighthouse, California (United States).

8-9 ■ Ar-Men Lighthouse, Finistère (France).

"THE ROCKY LEDGE RUNS FAR OUT INTO THE SEA
AND ON ITS OUTER POINT, SOME MILES AWAY,
THE LIGHTHOUSE LIFTS ITS MASSIVE MASONRY,
A PILLAR OF FIRE BY NIGHT, OF CLOUD BY DAY."

From "The Lighthouse"
Henry Wadsworth Longfellow (1807-1882)

The fascinating history of lighthouses reaches back into
the mists of time, in step with that of navigation.

Man discovered at a very early stage that he could move on water. The sea routes were multiplied and extended from the time of the Egyptians through to that of the Phoenicians, but ships still sailed prevalently close to the coast and during the day. When man learned how to use the stars for orientation, he started sailing at night too, and had to deal with rocks, sandbanks and currents. The earliest "lighthouses" date back to these times and were no more than bonfires situated in dangerous spots so that they could signal the route to ships. These first fires, which had to remain lit all night, required continuous attention: fuel, technical skill and constant human presence were all necessary. In Book XIX of the *Iliad*, Homer compares Achilles' gleaming shield to one of these fires: "[Achilles] took up the shield so great and strong that shone afar with a splendor as of the moon. As the light seen by sailors from out at sea, when men have lit a fire in their homestead high up among the mountains, but the sailors are carried out to sea…" Many other classical poets described lighthouses, inspired by the myth of the secret lovers Hero and Leander. Hero, a priestess of Aphrodite, would await her lover each night on the shore of the Hellespont, which he would swim to reach her, guided by her lighted torch. However, one night the wind extinguished the light and Leander was drowned; Hero, in her desperation, drowned herself too.

As commercial shipping developed and the first ports were built on the busiest shipping routes, bonfires were replaced with more powerful signaling equipment. One of the most famous, listed among the Seven Wonders of the World by Philon of Byzantium in the 2nd century BC, was the Colossus of Rhodes, an enormous statue of the sun god Helios, holding a lighted brazier in one hand. According to tradition, it was at least 70 cubits (ca. 105 feet) tall and was built astride the harbor, which the ships entered and left between its legs. Although historians disagree all the documents concur that the enormous sculpture was the work of Chares of Lindos, who build it in about 290 BC. However, the Colossus was short-lived, for it was toppled by an earthquake 80 years after its construction. A legend tells that its ruins were sold by the Arabs to a Jewish merchant in the 7th century, and that some of the parts ended up in Italy and were used for the construction of the famous statue of St. Charles Borromeo in Arona, on Lake Maggiore. The Colossus of Rhodes was not history's only anthropomorphic lighthouse. More recently, the Statue of Liberty was positioned at the entrance to Upper New York Bay as an aid to navigation, making it a lighthouse to all intents and purposes—despite its fixed light—run by the US Lighthouse Service. It was electrified soon after its erection. However, the quintessential lighthouse, and another of the Seven Wonders of the World, was that of Alexandria, the huge city founded by Alexander the Great in 332 BC on Egypt's Mediterranean coast. This lighthouse had a long but troubled life. It was built around 280 BC by Sostratus of Cnidus on the little island of Pharos (now a promontory) facing Alexandria, and was so renowned in the ancient world that the name of the island became synonymous with this kind of structure. It was built at the time of the Ptolemies, the pharaohs of Hellenistic Egypt and the last dynasty, which ended with Cleopatra and Roman rule. Construction commenced during the reign of Ptolemy I (305-283 BC), a former general of Alexander the Great, and was completed during that of his son, Ptolemy II (285-246 BC). It was the most famous lighthouse of antiquity. The 394-foot tower was clad with white stone and had an extraordinary range of over 30 miles, due to a system of mirrors that intensified the effect of the brazier positioned on its summit. Its square base was 233 feet tall and surmounted by a 79-foot octagonal middle section, which supported a cylindrical lantern with a statue of Zeus on the top. Inside the building, a wide ramp enabled the fuel (resinous wood) to be transported up to the lantern by mules. The tower also housed a garrison of soldiers who guarded the harbor. In AD 641 the lighthouse was damaged when the Arabs besieged the city. It was subsequently destroyed by a series of earthquakes.

In 1995, while searching the seafloor of Alexandria's harbor for traces of the ancient city, a team of French underwater archaeologists led by Jean Yves Empereur came across several enormous blocks of granite that appeared to belong to the base of the lighthouse. However, apart from monumental structures, antiquity witnessed the proliferation of simple bonfires, lit on coastal high points.

The Romans built the first towers with wood-burning braziers and exported the model for these structures from the restricted Mediterranean basin to all areas of the expanding Empire. In Italy, the Emperor Claudius built a port at Ostia in AD 50, which was subsequently extended to its present form by Trajan, to serve as Rome's coastal outlet. Its entrance was dominated by a lighthouse inspired by that of Alexandria, in appearance if not size, which can still be seen depicted in the mosaic floor of the Square of the Corporations in Ancient Ostia. Other similar buildings were erected wherever there was a Roman port, from the Tyrrhenian to the Adriatic. Before the fall of the Roman Empire, 30 signal towers lit the sea along the Mediterranean and Atlantic coasts. One lighthouse built by the Romans, at La Coruña, is still active after 2,000 years. It is known as the Tower of Hercules, due to the many legends that surround it, and was built by Caius Servius Lupus around the 1st century AD, during Trajan's rule. No trace, however, remains of another Roman lighthouse, built by Caligula around AD 41, on the French coast near Boulogne.

Charlemagne himself ordered its restoration in AD 800, and it was still lit occasionally, but later deteriorated until it finally collapsed in 1644.

Following the fall of Rome, even the sea was obscured during the ensuing Dark Ages. In England and France, which were already ruled by great dynasties, the role of lighthouses was chiefly entrusted to the towers of coastal monasteries. They were lit by fires fueled by wood, or simply by candles, and were run by monastic orders, hermit monks and the great knightly religious orders, such as the Templars, Hospitallers and Knights of Malta. In Germany, the Hanseatic League united many German and Scandinavian coastal cities and promoted the building of lighthouses to signal the coasts and ports. However, it was not until the 12th century, when trade was resumed with the East that several towers were built along the coasts of Italy. Fires were kept burning on their tops, fueled by heather and broom, the most common combustible materials. This period saw the construction Genoa and Porto Pisano lighthouses and the tower on the Meloria Shoals, as well as the renovation of the old Roman building of Capo Peloro in Messina. Of these, only the Genoa Lighthouse, rebuilt during the Renaissance, is still active today. Maintenance of harbor lighthouses was ensured by the duties that incoming ships had to pay for the upkeep and fueling of the fires on the tops of these towers. During the same period, the compass became widely adopted for navigation purposes, requiring the creation of maps and portolan charts, which also showed the position of signal points.

During Renaissance and Baroque times, lighthouses were considered architectural structures that required a certain degree of monumentality, just like any other important building. Late in the 16th century in France, Louis de Foix built the Cordouan Lighthouse in the style of a fairytale castle bristling with spires and pinnacles, while during the second half of the 17th century in England, the first Eddystone Lighthouse was constructed in the form of a bizarre wooden tower with a large open veranda, a terrace and an elaborate lantern. However, such handsome, refined architecture was often not capable of performing its task efficiently, and sometimes not even able to resist the fury of the sea. The 19th century was that of "pharology": while imaginative design and the love of beauty prevailed in France, several masterpieces of engineering were constructed along the coasts of England, Scotland and Ireland. Authentic dynasties of lighthouse builders erected severe and simple towers on rocks that hardly emerged above sea level, performing what appeared to be impossible feats. The Douglass family in England, the Stevensons in Scotland and the Halpins in Ireland invented granite structures that were built only just above the surface of the sea, but which were capable of resisting even the most terrible storms. Examples are the Skerryvore Lighthouse off thge Scottish coast and the fourth Eddystone Lighthouse off the English coast.

In North America too, the first European colonists felt the need to mark the coasts. Thirteen lighthouses had already been built by 1778, chiefly in New England. Although the American lighthouses were originally modeled on those of the Old World, they soon acquired their own distinctive style. Trade between East and West led to the construction of lighthouses all over the world. Towers were built wherever there was a European colony or Western ships sailed: from India to Japan (where the Scottish engineer Richard Henry Brunton built many lighthouses), China and beyond. Architectural and engineering developments were accompanied by technological advances. Stronger towers were equipped with increasingly efficient lights. Early lighthouses faced tough problems. Wood, which was undoubtedly the commonest and most easily available fuel, required constant stoking; coal did not provide enough light; wind constantly extinguished the flame and smoke obscured it, preventing good visibility. Glass appeared around 1200 and lighthouses assumed a more familiar form, with a lantern on the top that protected the fire. This improvement made it possible to use fuels other than wood, such as candles, wax, spermaceti (the precious wax extracted from the heads of sperm whales), olive oil or whale oil, according to latitude. However, the windows consisted of thick, opaque panes of glass, which were often obscured by soot. The thickness of the glass was not reduced until 1700, when its transparency also became similar to that used today. However, the light was still too dim.

In 1782 the Swiss physicist Aimé Argand (1755-1803) invented a circular burner with ten wicks fueled by oil, which lasted for ten days and was positioned so that the smoke was conveyed upward, making the light more visible. His burner crossed the Atlantic and was installed in the American lighthouses. Other scientific research had resulted in systems of parabolic reflectors that intensified the light: the most efficient of these was developed in the late 18th century by Jonas Norberg (1711-1783), who invented a type of lamp whose light was intensified by rotating mirrors, moved by a manual clockwork mechanism with counterweights. Norberg's device was used for many years, and is still adopted as an emergency system in many lighthouses. The French watchmaker Bertrand Carcel (1750-1812) further refined the Argand lamp with several concentric wicks. This lamp was also used for many years, until Fresnel his improved lenses. Augustin Jean Fresnel (1788-1827) was a civil engineer who studied the refraction of light. In 1822 he designed a lens that he successfully used in the lantern of Brittany's Cordouan Lighthouse the following year and that is currently housed in the Musée des Phares et Balises on Ouessant Island. This innovative lens is based on a simple principle: it has a slightly oval shape, and a series of prismatic (catadioptric) rings at the top and bottom reflect the rays of light towards the center, where they are they are concentrated by the main lens and beamed outwards.

These lenses were initially extremely heavy and it was very difficult to turn them. Fresnel himself solved the problem by placing them on floats in a mercury bath. Mercury is very dense, allowing it to support considerable weights while reducing friction to a minimum. However, mercury baths were gradually abandoned due to their toxicity, and were replaced with clockwork systems with counterweights until the advent of electric motors. Fresnel's lenses have been improved over the years and they are still used by lighthouses all over the world. The Scottish engineer Alan Stevenson, who built 12 lighthouses, also refined these lenses that were manufactured in England by Chance Brothers of Birmingham. The lamp fuel also changed: at the beginning of the 19th century, a gradual transition was made from oil, which was expensive and required constant monitoring, to coal gas, which was used for street lighting. Kerosene was extracted for the first time in 1859, in the United States, making kerosene oils—and paraffin-based ones in particular—available for lighthouses. In 1885 the Austrian chemist Carl Auer Welsbach (1858-1929) invented the incandescent gas mantle, which produced a very bright flame. The discovery in 1892 of acetylene, a compound of hydrogen and carbon, marked another turning point, enabling lighthouses to be built in the middle of the sea. The radiant power of acetylene was found to be far superior to that of all fuels previously employed, and cost much less, although its use required several precautions. Lighthouses gradually started to be electrified between the end of the 19th and the beginning of the 20th century. However, the process was only completed many years later. In locations where it was impossible to connect the towers to a supply grid, such as open-sea lighthouses, electrification was achieved by means of generators or alternative energy supplies, such as wind or solar power. The light bulbs have also been improved over the years, until the development of the 1000-watt halogen bulbs that now equip almost all lighthouses. Only a handful still use the old xenon bulbs, containing the inert, odorless and colorless noble gas discovered in 1898 by the English chemists William Ramsey and Morris W. Travers.

In our mind's eye, a lighthouse always has a keeper, who was an irreplaceable presence for many centuries and a figure midway between adventure and legend. The first keepers were probably slaves, who gathered and stacked the wood to be burned on the hills or in the braziers atop the towers from dusk to dawn. During the Middle Ages, the signal fires were fueled by monks, who perhaps considered it their sacred duty to feed the flames on the highest tower to signal the danger to passing ships. However, with the 19th-century multiplication of lighthouses as we know them, the figure of keeper—often accompanied by his family—changed greatly. The keeper was still essential for the technical maintenance of the lighthouse, and became a hero of a frontier world, between land and sea, overlooking a fascinating and terrible expanse, which was capable of assailing the foundations of even the strongest towers. A man with nerves of steel, who unconcernedly observed the most terrifying storms, listened fearlessly to the roar of the tempestuous ocean; the captain of a sailing ship without sails or helm, who resisted nature's fury armed with his willpower alone. Over the years, technological advances have eased the keepers' lives, lightening their workload, until making their presence unnecessary. The advent of photocells and remote-controlled computers have enabled their families to settle in houses far from the sea and the keepers themselves have turned into specialized technicians, who travel to the lighthouse by helicopter to perform routine maintenance operations. The solitude, heat, cold and dampness have now been forgotten, and the keepers are no longer at the center of adventurous stories and tedious reports, which convey the boredom of day after identical day, but also the thrill of extraordinary acts of heroism.

One story tells how the keeper of Portland Head Lighthouse, in Maine, improvised a rudimentary aerial ropeway from the top of the tower to the masts of a ship that had been wrecked on the rocks, managing to rescue its crew, with the help of his wife and children. Another recounts the tragedy of the keeper of the Eddystone Light-

16-17 ■ La Vieille Lighthouse, Brittany (France).
Inside the lantern.

18-19 ■ Punta della Guardia Lighthouse, island
of Ponza (Italy).

house, aged over 90 years old, who swallowed some molten lead that had fallen from the lantern as he was trying to extinguish a fire. He died a few days later. Another still narrates the fatal accident that claimed the life of the keeper of the Waugoshance Lighthouse, on Lake Michigan, who was walking along the landing jetty one evening in 1894, failed to see its end, and fell in the lake, where he drowned. A legend tells that his ghost still wanders amid the ruins of the lighthouse. The keeper of the Italian Marettimo Lighthouse, on the other hand, claimed that he lived with the ghosts of sailors who had died during the 1942 naval battle in the Strait of Messina (Italy), and set places at his table for them each day.

Life in the open-sea lighthouses, where the towers were shaken by the waves, supplies were scarce, and changeover very difficult, bordered on the limits of human endurance. In the 1930's, during a terrible storm that had cut off the island of Cavoli, southeast of Sardinia, from the mainland for days, the lighthouse keeper was forced to gather the bodies of the seagulls that had been dashed against the rocks by the wind in order to feed his family. It is still possible for a keeper to risk his life, in distant lighthouses, as witnessed during the tsunami that ravaged South East Asia on December 26, 2004: the wave swept away everything on Indira Point, the southernmost cape of India, saving only the lighthouse, which the rescuers found empty. Radar, LORAN (Long Range Aid to Navigation) and GPS (Global Positioning System) have given cargo ships and tankers far more effective instruments. However, lighthouses are not just signal towers. Sailors see them as the kindly eye of a friend, the light shining from the window of their home, their return, the hope of interrupting an overly long voyage, the sensation that danger is now behind them. For ordinary people a lighthouse is a civic monument, with a mysterious charm: an obelisk that speaks to the sea gods, a protective sentinel, a defensive bulwark. However, it is also a reassuring work of intellect, of the type that helps us to face the boundless forces of nature and instill faith in man's capacity.

Those who enjoy experiencing the emotions that historical buildings can absorb and transmit see lighthouses as stories to tell, real lives, shipwrecks, heroic acts, grim ghost stories, the wind whistling up the spiral stairs, the roar of the angry sea and the drumming of the rain on the windows. They are also an excellent source of inspiration for writers, from Jules Verne's *The Lighthouse at the End of the World*, to Virginia Woolf's *To the Lighthouse* and Sergio Bambarén's *The Guardian of the Light*.

What fate awaits lighthouses? Do they belong to an age without a present or a future, of which they will be mere mute souvenirs? Some will be sold to private individuals, who will convert them into homes, hotels or apartments. Others will be conserved so that the historical and human values epitomized by lighthouses may be handed down to posterity. Yet others will be kept active, at least until coastal shipping—pleasure boaters and fishermen—is able to count on totally reliable technological instruments. But even when all the boats in the world are equipped with computers and satellite receivers, how many will want to relinquish the reassuring sight of that kindly giant that watches over them and protects them from the coast?

THE TOWER OF
HERCULES

[LA CORUÑA ■ GALIZIA, SPAIN]

The Tower of Hercules is the world's oldest working lighthouse. Its appeal is enhanced by the numerous legends that surround it. The oldest of these attribute its construction to the mythical figure of Hercules, who is said to have erected the pillars marking the entrance to the Strait of Gibraltar.

However, the original tower was actually built during the rule of the Emperor Trajan, at the end of the first century A.D., by Caius Servius Lupus, an architect from Aeminium, close to modern-day Coimbra, in Portugal. It was consecrated to Mars, with the intention of being used as both a lighthouse and a watchtower for the defense of the nearby port of Brigantium, founded—accorded to another legend—by the Celtic leader Breogan and now known as

20 and 21 ■ La Coruña Lighthouse is surrounded by legends. One of these tells that it was built on the spot on which Hercules slew the three-bodied giant Geryon. The massive square tower of the lighthouse makes the lantern on the top seem small, although its beam is actually very powerful.

La Coruña, in Galicia. The lighthouse was built on a square plan with 59-foot sides and had three stories, each with four adjoining rooms. It was topped by a 13-foot cylindrical pinnacle that housed the braziers. The staircase was external and climbed to an overall height of 118 feet. The first time that the Tower of Hercules was called "Faro" (Spanish for "lighthouse", from Greek, after *Pharos*, the site of the ancient lighthouse at Alexandria, Egypt) was probably in a treatise by Paulus Orosius dated between 415 and 417 AD, and its use as a shipping beacon became increasingly associated with the nearby city and its environs. In 572 the name "Faro" was given to one of the territorial divisions donated to the diocese of Iria and in 830 the region was named the "Condado de Faro." When the inhabitants of the coast were forced to flee inland, from 846, following the Norman invasion, the new city founded by the refugees was called "Burgo de Faro." In his chronicles Saint Sebastian relates that the Normans arrived "as far as a spot known as Faro de Brigantium," in 1870. From 915 control of the city of "Farum Brigantium" passed to the diocese of Santiago de Compostela, whilst that of its peripheral territories, known as "Faro", remained divided between several monasteries and churches until King Bermudo II donated the "Condado de Faro" to the Church of Santiago in 991. During the Middle Ages, Alfonso V confirmed the donation of the county to the church, with the exception of the tower, which was fought over by several noble families, due

22 left ■ The original appearance of the rooms inside the lighthouse was maintained during renovation of the tower and the high vaults and stone arches reveal its ancient roots.

22 right ■ The inside of a lantern is always a special place. The lenses are housed in the center and a large window runs all around, overlooking the world. This particular window looks out over the Atlantic Ocean.

23 ■ The base of ancient La Coruña Lighthouse disappears in the fog in an evocative picture affording a glimpse of the extreme tip of the headland that closes the bay with the rocks below, beaten by the sea.

to its strategic position and solid construction, which made it an ideal fortress. Possession of the lighthouse subsequently returned to the crown and later to the diocese of Santiago de Compostela. All these changes had a detrimental effect on the state of preservation of the tower, which fell into decline due to inadequate maintenance. At the end of the 12th century Brigantium changed its name to La Coruña (from Latin *Ad columnam*, meaning "close to the pillar") and became the main city of the region during the following century. Nonetheless, the decline of the bastion continued and its external staircase was even demolished and its stones used to build a fortress inside the city. The building became the property of the city during the 16th century, but restoration was only commenced in 1682. Passages were created in the vaults of the rooms and an inside staircase was built in order to enable officials to reach the summit of the lighthouse. It was topped with two small towers to house the lanterns on the north side. The expenses for the repairs, reactivation and maintenance of the lighthouse were paid for ten years by the English, Dutch and Flemish consuls, who were concerned for the safety of shipping along all the coastal stretches crossed by their vessels. However, when this burden passed to the city authorities, it was followed by a new stage of decline. The monument was only revived in 1785, when the tower became the responsibility of the Galician Royal Maritime Consulate. During the same year its reconstruction was entrusted to Eustaqui Gianini, a naval officer and engineer, who clad the old core with 24-inch thick granite blocks and built an octagonal turret on the top and a new staircase inside. Work was completed in 1791, giving the lighthouse its current familiar appearance. The oil-burning lantern had seven reflectors and the eclipse was achieved by steel plates moved by a clockwork mechanism.

Only in the 20th century were important new innovations made: the old lighting systems were abandoned in 1921, when the lighthouse was electrified; a new keeper's house was built on the southwestern side of the base in 1956, and a foghorn and radio beacon were installed in the mid-1970s. The Tower of Hercules is still in service today and its signal consists of four flashes of white light with a duration of 20 seconds, visible at a distance of 23 miles.

LOCATION	COORDINATES	HEIGHT	RANGE	CONSTRUCTION
LA CORUÑA, GALICIA, SPAIN	43° 23' 9" N 8° 24' 24" W	157 FEET	23 MILES	1791

HOOK HEAD
LIGHTHOUSE

[HOOK POINT ■ IRELAND]

During the fifth century A.D. a monastic community led by Dubhán, (whose name in Irish means "fishing hook"), settled on a flat headland on the eastern coast of Ireland, not far from Hook Point. They founded a monastery on the site and, according to tradition, built a tower in 810 upon which a brazier was always kept burning to guide sailors. The history of the lighthouse on Hook Head (or Hook Point) resumed in 1172, when a Norman nobleman called Raymond LeGros built a lighthouse that was also a fortress on the same site of the ancient tower, entrusting to the monks of a nearby monastery the task of keeping the fire burning. In the Middle Ages it was not unusual for religious orders to be responsible for the maintenance of lighthouses and the monks of Hook Head continued their duty until the outbreak of the Civil War in 1641. The lighthouse's history is particularly closely related to the political events of England, which then ruled Ireland. The construction of lighthouses was not considered a priority in the Emerald Isle and during Cromwell's rule—the republican period of English and therefore Irish history—the one at Hook Head was abandoned, causing an increase in the number of shipwrecks along that stretch of coast. It was only after the Restauration, during the reign of Charles II, and after

24 ■ The Hook Head Lighthouse is a squat tower with black and white bands and is topped by a small lantern. It houses an architectural jewel that dates back to the Middle Ages.

25 ■ Hook Head Lighthouse is built on the stretch of rugged Irish coast that overlooks St. George's Channel, close to the former site of an ancient monastery.

several petitions, that the king ordered the construction of six new lighthouses along the Irish coast. The Hook Head Lighthouse was once again lit. The original tower was 60 feet high and 28 feet across, but during rebuilding its height was increased to 78 feet and its diameter to 40. An unusual and innovative feature for the period was the construction of a closed lantern on top of the tower, which protected the fire from the wind and conveyed the smoke upwards, making the light more visible. The stairs that led up to the lantern were built in the space between the old and new walls of the tower.

In 1704 Queen Anne transferred the management of the Irish lighthouses to the Treasury Commission, but the Hook Lighthouse was not included for it was privately rented and maintained this status. By the end of the 18th century the tower had fallen into a state of disrepair and the Commission entrusted Thomas Rogers with the task of restoring it. Rogers first of all installed a new 12-foot diameter lantern fitted with 12 Argand oil lamps. In 1812 the efficiency of the

lamps was improved and in 1864 other important changes were made to the lantern, with the installation of a fixed light with dioptric lenses. A cast-iron terrace was then placed on top of the tower to support the new lantern, and can still be seen today. The lantern was fueled by coal gas from 1871 to 1910, and switched to pressurized kerosene on January 1, 1911. A new optical system was installed on the same day: a revolving lens with a focal distance of 20 inches. A fog bell also operated between 1838 and 1995, which was adapted several times during the long years of service of the lighthouse, until being replaced with an intermittent electric signal. The alarm was accompanied by a white light during the night, which was switched off during the Second World War and reactivated in 1949. The lighthouse was electrified in 1972 and the intensity of its light was increased to 480,000 candle power, enabling the lantern to emit a beam of white light with a range of 23 miles every three seconds. The lighthouse was inhabited by its keepers' families up until 1977, when the keepers started alternating in solitary weekly shifts, like their colleagues who manned the open-sea lighthouses.

 26 top left ■ The old stone walls belonged to the first lighthouse that was built by a community of monks. The new lighthouse was built on top of this old building.

26 top right ■ The light is refracted in the Fresnel lenses of Hook Head Lighthouse, where an electric bulb projects its light for many miles.

27 top ■ A spiral fretted iron staircase leads up to the top of the tower.

LOCATION	COORDINATES	HEIGHT	RANGE	CONSTRUCTION
COUNTY WEXFORD, IRELAND	57° 7' N 6° 55' W	151 FEET	23 MILES	1172

Finally, the Hook Head Lighthouse was automated in 1996 and abandoned by its last keeper, although a technician returns regularly to check that everything is in perfect working order.

During its history the tower has changed color, from white with three red bands to white with two black bands in 1933. The lighthouse is not perfectly round, for it has a narrower turret above the second black band that supports the lantern. Its overall height is 115 feet (150 feet above sea level), although it still has a very solid appearance. It has an interesting stone interior, with high ceilings, arches, windows and an old fireplace that reveal its considerable age and hark back to the times of the monks and the Norman nobleman who had ordered it to be built.

26-27 ■ Near the coast, the rolling Irish countryside becomes a mass of rocks, representing a hazard for shipping. This bird's-eye view shows Hook Head Lighthouse reaching out towards the Irish Sea, firmly rooted in the great rocks swept by the waves.

LA LANTERNA

[LIGURIA ■ ITALY]

"La Lanterna" is the symbol of the city of Genoa and has seven centuries of history extending back to its misty origins. The lighthouse is mentioned in a decree dated 1129 that entrusted is supervision to the people of Genoa: this first tower was probably built around 1128 on a rock rising out of the sea in a place known as Capo di Faro (Lighthouse Cape). The light was provided by a fire fueled by dry stems of heather (*brugo*) and broom (*brisca*), which were constantly added to its summit in order to signal the port entrance. Certain 12th-century documents show that painstaking attention was paid to the care and maintenance of the tower and that every ship entering the port of Genoa had to pay duties *pro igne facendo in capite Fari*. A succession of maritime authorities have been responsible for the management of the Lanterna over the centuries: the *Consoli del Mare* (Sea Consuls), *Salvatori del Porto* (Saviors of the Port), *Padri del Comune e Salvatori del Porto* (Fathers of the Commune and Saviors of the Port) and the *Conservatori del Mare* (Keepers of the Sea). Their records make it easy to reconstruct the history of the Genoa Lighthouse. In 1316 the tower officially became a lighthouse. Caught up in the war between the Guelphs and Ghibellines, its foundations were damaged in 1318, and reinforced in 1321. The first lantern

28   A *View of Genoa in 1481*, housed in the Pegli Naval Museum (Genoa). The painting by Cristoforo De Grassi dates back to the 16th century and is a reproduction of a much older work, although in 1481 the lighthouse did not yet have the form shown here.

29   The Genoese are very fond of the Lanterna. During the night it is illuminated with lights that make it visible for many miles. The 14th-century frescoed coat of arms on the northern side of the tower was restored in 1991.

was fueled by olive oil and installed in 1326, as recorded by the Genoese historian Giustiniani.

The first depiction of the Lanterna dates back to 1371 and takes the form of a pen drawing on the cover of a handbook belonging to the *Salvatori del Porto* that was also used to record the expenses for the illumination of the lighthouse and the appointment of its keepers. Around 1400 the lighthouse was used as a prison, whose inmates included James of Lusignan and his wife Heloïse, who gave birth to their son Janus in a small room. In 1405 the lighthouse keepers were priests, explaining why the tower was topped with the Christian symbols of a fish and a cross; eight years later a decree issued by the "*Consoli del Mare*" allocated "36 Lire" to the management of the lighthouse, which had come to be considered essential for the safety of shipping. The Lanterna was struck by lightning twice, in 1481 and 1602, causing damage to its upper part. It is said that in 1449 one of the lighthouse keepers was Antonio Colombo, Christopher Columbus' paternal uncle. In 1507 Louis XII of France ordered the construction of the fort known as the Briglia at the foot of the lighthouse, which was besieged by Andrea Doria's army five years later, when the tower was cut in half by cannon fire during the battle. The new lighthouse was built on this stump in 1543, commissioned by the Doge Andrea Centurione and financed by the Bank of San Giorgio. A gruesome legend relates that the anonymous architect who had designed the Lanterna was thrown off its top following its completion, so that he could never build another the same. In 1543 the Lanterna assumed its current form and was topped by a new dome. A handwritten 16th-century pilot's book recounts: "Fourteen miles from Peggi (Pegli), a city with an excellent port, there is a very high lantern in the western part that signals to the ships at its feet," whose light could already be seen from a great distance. The lighthouse keepers, known as

30-31 ■ The Genoa Lighthouse was built on a rock on the seashore. However, due to the extension of the port and construction of the airport, it is now located considerably farther back, on dry land. This eastward view shows it towering above the terminals and quays.

31 ■ The Fresnel lenses of the Genoa Lighthouse surround a 1,000-watt halogen bulb. Its light is amplified by the lenses and can be seen for many miles.

turrexani della torre, were required to dedicate great care to the maintenance and cleaning of the glass parts. Between 1711 and 1791 a lightning rod was installed to avoid further damage during storms, tie-rods and bolts were added to strengthen the building, and its foundations were reinforced. Fresnel lenses, were installed in 1843, extending the range of the lighthouse beam to 15 miles. In 1898 the lighting power was further increased by the introduction of acetylene gas, which was replaced by pressurized kerosene in 1904 until being supplanted by electricity in 1936. Over the following years an electrical motor took the place of the old hand-wound clockwork system and

LOCATION	COORDINATES	HEIGHT	RANGE	CONSTRUCTION
GENOA, LIGURIA, ITALY	44° 25' N 8° 56' E	252 FEET	26 MILES	1543

the mercury bath revolving mechanism was replaced with another on ball bearings. An independent spare light was also installed. Today the majestic Lanterna dominates the port and city from a height of over 250 feet: the waves no longer break on the rocks at its feet, as its surroundings have undergone extensive change with the construction of new quays and an airport. However, it offers incomparable views over Genoa and the Ligurian Riviera to those who venture up its 365 stairs and casts its beam over 26 miles of dark sea every night.

THE CORDOUAN
LIGHTHOUSE

[GARONNE ▪ FRANCE]

A historic lighthouse illuminates the waters of the Gironde Estuary, on the western coast of France, not far from the city and port of Bordeaux. The Cordouan Lighthouse is the oldest in France. A legend recounts that a primitive building was constructed during the 9th century by Charlemagne's son, Louis the Pious, five miles beyond the Gironde Estuary. It is certain that there was a tower in the years around 1360, built by Edward, Prince of Wales—known as the Black Prince—the son of Edward III of England that occupied part of France during the late Middle Ages. The construction had been requested by the Spanish merchants of the city of Cordova, then under Moorish rule, requested the construction. They shipped leatherware to this area of France and returned home laden with Bordeaux wines. The original polygonal tower was 52 feet tall and the wood fire on its top was

32 ▪ The two lighthouse keepers at the windows of the ancient lantern, beneath the elaborate iron dome. The Fresnel lenses are clearly visible behind them.

33 ▪ Today Le Cordouan Lighthouse is a solitary obelisk at the entrance to the Gironde River. This is all that remains of the fairytale castle that was built by Louis de Foix in 1611.

kept burning by a hermit, who survived on the charity of passing ships. Although the practice of requesting dues was new for France, it was not unusual in other parts of Europe, such as Genoa. The name of the lighthouse is also surrounded by legend. It seems as though "Cordouan" was originally "Cordovan", which derived from the fact that it had been built to increase trade with the Spanish city of Cordova.

In 1495 fires were also kept burning on the tower in daytime to warn of the presence of enemies to approaching ships. In this case they could find refuge in the port of La Rochelle or other nearby safe havens. The tower was gradually ruined by the force of the waves and the strong Atlantic winds, and a series of shipwrecks ensued. The rulers of Guyenne, an ancient region of southwestern France belonging to the Duchy of Aquitaine, urged the rebuilding of the tower on several occasions, requesting the intervention of King Henry II and Catherine de' Medici, but their pleas went unanswered. It was only during the reign of Henry III, in 1584, that the bare tower commenced the transformation that was to make it one of the wonders of the modern world. During that year, the architect Louis de Foix, who had worked on the construction of the Escorial in Spain, was commissioned to design a new lighthouse. Louis de Foix realized that the old tower could no longer be used and so demolished it. He then set about designing a new, tall and imposing lighthouse. However, enormous difficulties were encountered during its construction. The islet on which the foundations had been built started to be submerged by the sea, requiring the immediate construction of a tall

34-35 ■ The Gironde Estuary opens on to the Bay of Biscay, which is scoured by the tides of the Atlantic Ocean. During high tide the lighthouse is completely cut off from dry land, while at low tide it can be reached by the narrow jetty used by the keepers at changeover time.

35 top ■ The lighthouse's magnificent chapel was built in pure Baroque style. In the center is a strange stone tank, a well, which is connected to all the floors of the lighthouse.

35 bottom ■ The interior of Le Cordouan Lighthouse is perfectly cylindrical and a long spiral staircase rises around the outer wall. The well-head in the chapel can be seen in the center.

cofferdam. The impressive structure was only completed by de Foix's son and his master mason in 1611, 27 years after it had been commenced.

The result was an imposing monument, combining the styles of a fortress, a church and a palace: a little Versailles in the middle of the sea. The lighthouse was 121 feet tall, with a smooth, round base built in Renaissance style, and a magnificent entrance topped by a statue of Neptune that led to a hall giving onto the keepers' quarters. The floor above houses the pure Baroque-style apartments of the king and his lieutenant. Higher still is the chapel—now deconsecrated—whose entrance features two marble plaques dated 1665 and 1727, presented by Kings Louis XIV and Louis XV to commemorate changes made to the lighthouse during their reigns. The structure was topped by a small tower that housed the decorated lantern and was surmounted by a tall pinnacle. The outer appearance of the lighthouse, adorned with columns with

LOCATION	COORDINATES	HEIGHT	RANGE	CONSTRUCTION
GIRONDE ESTUARY, FRANCE	43°35" N 1° 10" W	187 FEET	22 MILES	1611

Doric and Corinthian capitals, sculptures and pinnacles, earned the building the unusual title of "Le Roi des phares, le phare des Rois." The range of the lantern was not very great, but it should be remembered that the Cordouan Lighthouse was the product of an age in which beauty was considered more important than usefulness. Nonetheless, the construction was relatively short-lived. In 1789 the engineer Joseph Teulère, who had designed Bordeaux's port, rebuilt the lighthouse, demolishing the dome of the chapel and the lantern and raising the structure to a height of 187 feet. At the end of the 18th century the lighthouse was fueled by whale, rapeseed and olive oil. In 1790 it had been equipped with a revolutionary lighting system, featuring 30 oil-burning lamps and reflectors moved by a weight, which enabled the light to be rotated for the first time. Such devices had been invented and tried out over the years with the purpose of increasing the range of lighthouses, thus preventing their lights from being confused with

those of the coast. The technique used for the Cordouan Lighthouse was invented by Jonas Norberg (1711-1783), who had increased the number of wicks to achieve a more powerful beam. In 1823 the lantern was fitted with Fresnel lenses, which had recently been invented by the French physicist Augustine Fresnel (1788-1827), and immediately after the Second World War, the lighthouse was equipped with its first generator. Over the centuries the tower has lost its Baroque charm, becoming an obelisk in the middle of the sea. Today it is a modern lighthouse, but the lower part, the first floor and the interior with the royal apartments and chapel with original windows have remained just as Louis de Foix built them.

36-37 ■ The red and green sectors of the lantern are clearly visible when the keepers switch on the lantern.

PORTLAND BILL

[DORSET ■ GREAT BRITAIN]

The county of Dorset is situated in southern England. Its inland territory is mainly wooded, rolling countryside, whilst its rugged coasts overlook the English Channel. The Isle of Portland is located in the southern part of the county. It is linked to the mainland by a bridge and its extreme tip is home to the Portland Bill Lighthouse.

This very exposed site has been the scene of numerous shipwrecks, caused by the meeting of the tides and the strong currents. As early as the second half of the 17th century, a certain John Clayton was commissioned to erect a lighthouse on the southernmost tip of the Isle of Portland, but for some mysterious reason it was never built. At the beginning of the 18th century Captain William Holman, backed by the people nearby Weymouth, presented a petition to the

38 ■ The tower is emblazoned with the coat of arms of Trinity House, the English lighthouse authority that has always been directly accountable to the Crown.

39 ■ The elegant red and white tower of Portland Bill Lighthouse is topped by a great white lantern, protected by a metal grille.

40-41 ■ In 1844 a white stone obelisk was erected on the red rocks where the lighthouse stands as a further signal for sailors on the sea below.

41 ■ A metal ladder, allowing access to the roof for maintenance, juts out from the glowing lantern silhouetted against the pink sky.

lighthouse authority, Trinity House, for the realization of the project. However, it was rejected as it was considered needless and difficult to maintain a lighthouse in such a location. In 1716 Trinity House obtained a patent from George I for the construction of the lighthouse. The authority in turn issued a lease for 61 years to a private consortium that built not one, but two lighthouses. However, the venture was not a success, for the lighthouses were neglected and often not lit at all, as revealed by a report made by members of the Board of Trinity House, following an inspection in 1752.

Upon expiry of the lease the lighthouses reverted to Trinity House. In 1789 William Johns, a Weymouth builder under contract to Trinity House, demolished one of the towers and erected a new one at a cost of £2,000. It was the first lighthouse in England to be fitted with the new Argand lamps with reflectors, as an inscription over the doorway recalls.

In 1798, when Napoleon threatened to invade Eng-

land, two 18-pound cannors were installed near the lighthouse to defend the coast.

In 1844 the 23-foot stone obelisk that still stands on the southernmost tip of the island was erected as a daytime warning to ships of the dangerous rocky reef extending almost 100 feet south into the sea.

In 1869 the tower was rebuilt and had the honor of a royal visit from George III. The old lighthouse built in 1716 was sold to private buyers in the early 1920s and had a succession of different owners before being abandoned. It remained almost in ruins until another private purchaser bought it in 1981, when it was completely renovated. The building that was once the fuel store is now rented out to those wishing to try the experience of staying next to a lighthouse.

At the beginning of the 20th century Trinity House cnnounced its intention to replace the old towers with a single one, and the Portland Bill Lighthouse as we know it today was lit in 1906. The tapered tower is 135 feet tall and topped

Location	Coordinates	Height	Range	Construction
PORTLAND ISLE, DORSET, GREAT BRITAIN	50° 30' N 02° 27' W	135 FEET	25 MILES	1716

with a tall metal lantern, reached by an internal staircase of 153 steps.

The entire structure is painted white, with a red band halfway up the tower. Two white buildings stand at its base, which once served as a keepers' house and a store for fuel and equipment. The lantern has an unusual feature: its optical system has been arranged so that the character gradually changes from one to four white flashes between the bearings 221° and 224° and from four to one white flash between bearings 117° and 141°.

The lighthouse was automated on March 18, 1996, when monitoring and control of the station was transferred to the control center at Harwich.

The old tower is still standing and has become a bird observatory.

42-43 ■ The lighthouse dominates the southern tip of the Isle of Portland, in an area of sea characterized by rocks and currents that are a serious hazard to shipping.

FORTE STELLA
LIGHTHOUSE

[PORTOFERRAIO, ELBA ■ ITALY]

The island of Elba is a scrap of Tuscan land in the Tyrrhenian Sea, off the northwest coast of Italy. The island was already inhabited in remote times and was subsequently colonized by the Etruscans and the Romans, who quarried granite, mined the island's rich ore deposits and called its most important town Fabricia. At the beginning of the 11th century the island came under Pisan rule, becoming part of Tuscany. The name Elba appears to have been documented for the first time during this period. The main town is now known as Portoferraio, although this name was only coined in the 18th century. In 1500 the island became part of the Principality of Piombino and the Grand Duke Cosimo I de' Medici changed the name of ancient Fabricia to Cosmopolis and built great fortifications around it, designed to make it impenetrable to attack. Between 1548 and 1549 the architects Bellucci and Camerini built the Linguella and Attacco forts either side of the city, which were connected by bastions to the complexes of Forte Stella and Forte Falcone to the north. These walls were so mighty that not even the fierce pirate Turgut, better known as Dragut, the terror of the Mediterranean, dared attack them. After having been divided between the Spanish, French and the Medici family, in 1700 the island—and the whole of Tuscany—came under the rule of the house of Lorraine and its capital assumed its current name of Portoferraio.

In 1778 the Archduke Leopold of Lorraine built an 82-foot round tower on the northern bastion of Forte Stella. The style of the structure was vague-

44 and 44-45 ■ The massive stone tower that rises against the sky on the western side of Forte Stella in Portoferraio was built under the rule of the House of Lorraine in 1778 and is now the lighthouse that marks the entrance to the city's port.

ly medieval, with crenellations beneath the lantern, whose signal was merely intended to greet ships entering the roadstead. In 1860 the island became part of united Italy. In 1862 a permanent signal was installed on the tower. The lighthouse is now electrified and features a fixed optical unit that emits three white flashes every 14 seconds and has a range of 16 miles. Beneath the lantern is a red light that indicates the dangerous shallows off Capo Bianco. The Forte Stella Lighthouse is classified as a "landing lighthouse," a term that has nothing to do with aviation, but instead refers to the lanterns that mark the entrance to an important port or a specific route followed by ships.

This lighthouse is associated with a famous historical figure, for it was undoubtedly part of his surroundings for at least nine months of his life. Napoleon Bonaparte arrived in Portoferraio in exile on May 4, 1814 and settled in the Palazzina dei Mulini, in a splendid panoramic position between Forte Stella and Forte Falcone, making it his official residence and palace.

Location	Coordinates	Height	Range	Construction
Portoferraio, Elba, Italy	42° 49' N 10° 20' E	82 FEET (207 FEET ABOVE SEA LEVEL)	16 MILES	1778 (1862)

PORTLAND HEAD

LIGHTHOUSE

[MAINE ■ UNITED STATES]

46-47 ■ A stormy sky and waves breaking on the rocks create a romantic atmosphere around the lighthouse and the keeper's house, whose white forms seem to disappear into the fog.

The state of Maine was still part of Massachusetts in 1786, the year of the first appeal to build a lighthouse at the entrance to Portland Harbor. The city, known as Falmouth at the time, was one of the busiest ports in America. A shipwreck hastened construction, which began in 1787 but came to a halt almost immediately due to lack of funds. In 1789, when George Washington became president of the United States, Congress appropriated $1,500 to complete construction of the lighthouse. The work was to be done economically and, according to the original plans, the tower was supposed to be just 55 feet tall. By the time the work was finished, however, the structure was 72 feet tall. The lighthouse was first activated on January 10, 1791 and its lighting system relied on 16 lamps powered by whale oil.

The first keeper of Portland Head, a veteran of the Revolutionary War, was personally appointed by the President. He was not paid a salary, but was allowed to live in the annexed house, fish and plant a vegetable patch.

Exposed to the storms and winds of the Atlantic, by 1810 the lighthouse already needed repair work and ongoing maintenance. In 1813, Lewis lamps were installed in 1813. These were named after Winslow Lewis, a controversial sea captain who took the mechanism already used in European lighthouses and applied it to American ones. The poet Henry Wadsworth Longfellow, a native of

49 ■ This tapering tower was one of the first
American-style lighthouses built following the American
Revolution.

Portland, was a frequent visitor to Portland Head during this period and wrote his poem "The Lighthouse" as he sat on a rock at the base of the construction. There is now a plaque commemorating the poet.

Between 1850 and 1855, other lanterns were installed, the tower was clad with brickwork and a metal spiral staircase was installed inside. In 1864, the wreck of the *Bohemian*, a British steamship carrying immigrants from Liverpool, led to the decision to increase the height of the tower by 20 feet and install a Fresnel lens in order to enhance the lighting power of the lantern.

Former sea captain Joshua Strout, a native of Cape Elizabeth, became the lighthouse keeper in 1869, and this marked the beginning of a dynasty of keepers that was to last for 59 years, until 1928. One of the most mysterious shipwrecks in history took place during this period. On Christmas Eve of 1886, the three-masted bark *Annie C. Maguire* ran aground on the rocks directly beneath Portland Head. Aided by volunteers, Joshua, his wife and son extended an ordinary ladder from the shore to the ship, rescuing the captain, his wife, the officials and all the members of the crew. The cause of the shipwreck was never discovered: although it was winter, visibility was excellent and the sea was calm. All the valuables aboard were saved, and on New Year's Day of 1887 a storm completely destroyed the ship. This event is commemorated by these words painted on the seawall at the base of the lighthouse: "In memory of the ship Annie C. Maguire, wrecked here, December 24, 1886." The tower subsequently underwent further changes. The height of the tower—that was now 80 feet tall—was lowered by 20 feet in 1882, only to be increased again by 20 feet the following year. Electricity was brought to the lighthouse in 1929, and its light has only been turned off during the three middle years of the Second World War. Electrification of the lantern was the only technological innovation at Portland Head until 1989, when the equipment was automated. In 1990 the property was leased to the city of Cape Elizabeth, to which it was donated three years later through the efforts of Senator George Mitchell. Though the city of Cape Elizabeth continues to handle the administrative aspects, the Coast Guard is responsible for the actual running of the lighthouse.

The place that inspired Longfellow's poetry is now one of the most popular and photographed landmarks in America. The lighthouse, one of the oldest in the New World, is located in Fort Williams Park, and it offers visitors an enchanting view: its conical white tower, the two-story keeper's house, its red roofs, its black-painted iron lantern, and an unforgettable view of the ocean. In 1992 the keeper's house was converted into a museum and souvenir shop, and the rooms in the house are open to visitors. The tower, which is closed to the public, has stood here for over 200 years, the silent witness to all the historic events that have occurred at its feet.

Location	Coordinates	Height	Range	Construction
Portland, Maine United States	43° 37' N 70° 13' W	80 feet	24 miles	1791

FANAD HEAD
LIGHTHOUSE

[FANAD HEAD ■ IRELAND]

A small windswept headland stands high above the sea, reaching out into the Atlantic Ocean, on the northern coast of Ireland. This spot used to be called Fannet Point, although over the years it has become popularly known as Fanad Head.

50 ■ The red terrace and white tower contrast with Ireland's deep blue sea. The lighthouse, situated in a normally storm-ravaged area, looks less dramatic on a sunny day.

51 ■ Fanad Head Lighthouse was built in the 19th century to improve the safety along Ireland's rugged rocky coast, which represented a serious threat to shipping during the age of sail.

In 1812 the frigate *Saldana* was wrecked in the waters off the headland and lost her entire crew. This event emphasized the urgent need to build a lighthouse that would prevent new tragedies. The Royal Navy sent an official request to the local authorities, which was granted relatively quickly, and the construction of a lighthouse on Fannet Point was authorized in 1814. The task of designing and building the structure was entrusted to the maritime engineer George Halpin, who was later joined and eventually replaced by his son in the construction of over 50 lighthouses.

The Fannet Point lantern was first lit on March 17, 1817, and was considered an open-sea lighthouse—despite the fact that it is actually situated on a cliff

Location	Coordinates	Height	Range	Construction
Lough Swilly, County Donegal, Ireland	55° 16' N 7° 37' W	128 feet	14 miles	1817

marking the entrance to Lough Swilly, which almost forms a natural harbor. Its fixed light showed red to sea and white toward the Lough, and could be seen for 14 miles in clear weather. The lantern was equipped with a 9-burner Argand lamp, fueled by whale oil, and a parabolic reflector. As the waters around the headland were very dangerous, other lighthouses were built nearby and at the beginning of the 1880s it was decided to improve Fanad Head with the construction of another tower close to the existing one. The new building was fitted with a second-order dioptric lens and extra houses for the keepers were also built.

Other changes were made over the years, culminating in the electrification of the lighthouse, followed by its automation in 1975. In 1969 Fanad Head was chosen as one of the main helicopter bases for the maintenance of the open-sea lighthouses.

The lighthouse is situated on an imposing rock and is 72 feet tall (128 feet above sea level). Its white tower terminates in a red terrace beneath the lantern and is surrounded by several buildings constructed to house its keepers. Today the lighthouse is inhabited by a technician whose sole task is to monitor the functioning of the signaling equipment.

52-53 ■ The lighthouse is built on a green plateau on the edge of the cliff, surrounded by the keepers' houses.

53 top ■ The romantic and evocative lighthouse disappears into the darkness, flashing its beam of light across the sea.

53 bottom ■ The cliff falls sheer to the sea, 55 feet below the lighthouse.

THE CAPE ARKONA

LIGHTHOUSES

[RÜGEN ■ GERMANY]

Cape Arkona is situated on Rügen, the largest German island, which is connected to the mainland by a bridge. The capital of the island is Bergen, which looks out over the Baltic Sea towards Scandinavia. Rügen is about 30 miles across and boasts a wide variety of landscapes: wooded hills alternate with grassy meadows in the interior and the rocks, bays and little inlets of the coast are interrupted by broad sandy beaches. The island still bears the traces of the presence of ancient peoples in remote ages, as attested by megalithic tombs, and was also the scene of battles between Germanic tribes and their Scandinavian neighbors up until the Christianization of the region.

The northernmost tip of the island is home to two lighthouses. Although they stand close together, they were built during different periods and have different histories. The first and oldest was built as a navigation aid by the architect Karl Friedrich Schinkel in 1827. It has a square brick base that recalls the form of Nordic fortifications, while the multistory classical-style tower is dotted with rectangular windows and topped by battlements that ring a terrace supporting a simple round

54 ■ The Cape Arkona lighthouses stand on the northernmost coast of the island of Rügen, in the Baltic Sea. Both lighthouses can be seen in the photograph: the low square one is the oldest.

55 ■ The second Cape Arkona Lighthouse was built at the beginning of the 20th century to remedy the shortcomings of the old one, which was too low and not powerful enough.

56 top ■ The old Cape Arkona Lighthouse can be seen in this 19th-century print. The all-masonry tower built in 1827 had three stories resting on a square base and surmounted by a round lantern.

56 center and bottom ■ The lighting power of the 19th-century tower was limited. These drawings show the lenses used to refract light within the lantern.

56-57 ■ The new lighthouse and the lantern of the old one stand out against the summer sky of Mecklenburg-West Pomerania in this striking twilight view. The tower built in 1902 is more conventional in style. It has a round plan, a height of 115 feet and a range of over 24 miles, making it far better suited to the difficult weather conditions of the German Baltic coast.

Location	Coordinates	Height	Range	Construction
Island of Rügen, Germany	54° 41' N 13° 26' E	115 feet (Old Cape Arkona: 62 feet)	24 miles (Old Cape Arkona: 20 miles)	1902 (Old Cape Arkona: 1827)

lantern. The lighthouse is 62 feet tall and its light had a range of approximately 20 miles before it was deactivated. However, it was neither tall enough nor powerful enough for the requirements of the Baltic Sea. Early in the 20th century it was decided to build another tower instead of renovating it. The new lighthouse was built between 1901 and 1902, and was officially inaugurated on April 1, 1905, following a three-year trial period. The new building has a more conventional appearance than the old one. The 115-foot round tower rests on a broader base that supports its weight. Two terraces surrounded by iron railings are situated beneath the red-painted lantern with its pagoda roof. The height and powerful beam of the lighthouse (whose lantern has a range of 24 miles) have long made it a landmark of the Baltic coast.

The two lighthouses were recently declared national monuments and the entire area is now public property. The regional authorities and the "Friends of Cape Arkona" association organize various kinds of events there in order to raise the funds required for the maintenance of the buildings. The oldest lighthouse also houses the Maritime Museum.

BERLENGA
LIGHTHOUSE

[ESTREMADURA ■ PORTUGAL]

58-59 ■ A deep natural cave extends beneath the little island of Berlenga Grande and can be explored by boat along its entire length. The remains of a medieval fort are still visible beneath the little lighthouse.

The rocky Berlenga Islands—also known as the *Farilhões, Estelas,* and *Forcades*—emerge from the sea off the coast of the Portuguese region of Estremadura, about 60 miles north of Lisbon. The largest of the group, Berlenga Grande, is almost a mile long, half a mile wide and 275 feet high. This pink granite island is a nature reserve for migratory birds, which carpet it with their feathers toward the end of spring, creating the effect of a late snowfall. A natural cave, known as the Furado Grande, extends beneath the rocky surface.

The island is home to the medieval Forte de São João Batista, which was built by the monks who inhabited this remote spot to pray, meditate and—it seems—help sailors in peril. Frequent pirate raids led the monks to build a small fort on a neighboring islet, which was connected to the large island by a bridge. This structure was destroyed in 1666, when it was bombarded by 15 Spanish ships, it was rebuilt at the end of the 17th century.

Although Portugal started to become a maritime and colonial power from the 15th century, it did not seem to consider it necessary to light its coasts for many hundreds of years, despite the fact that they were exposed to the full fury of the Atlantic Ocean. Moreover, the loss of independence the result-

LOCATION	COORDINATES	HEIGHT	RANGE	CONSTRUCTION
ESTREMADURA, PORTUGAL	39° 24' N 09° 30' W	72 FEET (397 FEET ABOVE SEA LEVEL)	27 MILES	1836

60-61 ■ Other Portuguese lighthouses have a similar structure to that of Berlenga. The square shape, stone corners and red lantern are recurrent motifs of the Portuguese style.

61 ■ The imposing lighting system that has been housed in the lantern since the end of the 19th century is capable of projecting a powerful beam with a range of 27 miles.

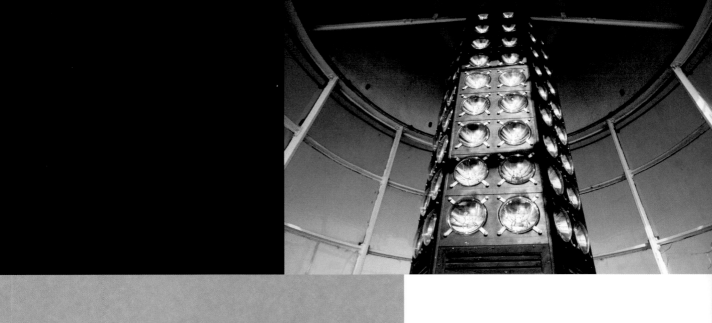

ed from Spain's annexation of the country (1580-1640) and the Napoleonic Invasion (1807-1811) made it more important to defend the coasts, rather than aid the approach of enemies by building lighthouses. Nonetheless, several monastic communities sporadically tended fires along the shore with the purpose of guiding sailors. However, in most cases the tending of fires was not followed by the building of masonry structures. For example, the first Portuguese lighthouse, Cabo Montedor, was commissioned in 1758, but was only lit for the first time over a century later. Although Portugal's coastline extends for 516 miles, it has just 25 lighthouses—far fewer than any other European country.

The Berlenga Lighthouse was built in 1836 on the highest end of the island by the engineers Guadencio Fontana and André Proença Vieira. The square stone tower is 72 feet high (397 feet above sea level) and is almost completely white, except for the gray corners of the structure and the red-painted metal lantern. The tower is surrounded by a series of low buildings housing the keepers' quarters and the equipment necessary for the operation of the lighthouse. In 1897 the lantern was fitted with an optical unit featuring hyper-radiant Fresnel lenses that still continue to emit three white flashes every 20 seconds, with a range of 27 miles. The lighthouse was electrified in 1985.

CABO MAYOR

LIGHTHOUSE

[SANTANDER ■ SPAIN]

The city of Santander , the regional capital of Cantabria, has always been an important port. It owes its riches to the heavy traffic of goods and people that reached its peak in the 16th century, with the export of Spanish wool to Flanders. The city is located on the edge of Santander Bay, which forms a natural harbor on Spain's northern coast and opens onto the Bay of Biscay and the Atlantic Ocean. Access to the bay is difficult due to the presence of several small islands and a sandbank, which straitens its entrance. Entry is also made perilous by the dominant westerly winds and the frequent storms that scour the Cantabrian coastline, especially during the winter.

A signal tower has stood on Cabo Mayor—a little headland west of the entrance to the bay—since ancient times. During stormy nights a fire was lit on its top to guide the fishing boats home (flags were used for signaling during the day). However, this system was not sufficient for the needs of modern and rapidly increasing maritime traffic. In 1776 a Spanish businessman requested permission to build a lighthouse on the headland, offering to run it in exchange for the transit duties collected from incoming ships. However, permission was denied and the entire area of Cabo Mayor remained unlit.

The project was reexamined two years later, when the authorities proposed a signal-

Location	Coordinates	Height	Range	Construction
Santander, Cantabria, Spain	43°29' N 3°47' W	98 feet	21 miles	1839

62-63 ■ The Cabo Mayor lighthouse's squat white tower rises above a sheer cliff that plunges into the sea. This sentinel has protected the entrance to Santander's port for over 160 years.

ing plan for the bay and port of Santander that was to be funded by the Royal Treasury. However, the area of Cabo Mayor was excluded because of its distance from the port. Both of the two plans that were considered both featured the construction of a lighthouse at the mouth of the bay, situated on the sandbank that narrowed its entrance, but tall enough to be seen from the sea on the other side of Cabo Mayor; or the building of a fortress topped by a lighthouse, which could defend the city while lighting the surrounding sea. However, both projects were abandoned for unknown reasons.

During the 19th century, trade with the Americas led to great changes in the city: its population grew, its port and shipyards expanded and the construction of a signal tower became essential and could no longer be postponed. In 1833 the Harbor Authority decided to build a lighthouse on Cabo Mayor—to be funded by duties levied on ships—in exactly the same spot chosen in 1776, which is still home to the building today. The lighthouse was solemnly inaugurated on August 15, 1839, with a lantern-lighting ceremony accompanied by popular songs and dances. The tower was covered in small paper flags, probably to recall the ancient lighthouse that used to show fisherman the way during the day. The lantern was lit by three circular oil-burning wicks, whose light was augmented by a system of reflectors. The optical system featured eight lenses and 100 mirrors in the upper part and 60 mirrors in the lower part to amplify the light. In those days the lantern burned approximately seven ounces of oil per hour. However, the presence of this imposing sentinel did not prevent a great marine tragedy from striking Santander: in 1893 the freighter *Cabo Machichaco* exploded in the port, killing over 500 men and causing serious damage to shore facilities.

64-65 ■ The large circular area at the base of the lighthouse is flanked by an ancient signal tower (left) and the low buildings used for storage (center), which were once the keepers' quarters.

65 ■ The lenses inside the lantern allow a glimpse of the two electric bulbs that were used to replace the obsolete oil burners upon electrification of the lighthouse.

The lighthouse has been altered many times over the years, but its structure has remained true to the original. Only the lantern has undergone changes, due to technological developments. The most important of these was electrification in 1920, followed by the installation of a modern fog signal in 1954 and a radio beacon in 1958.

The imposing 98-foot white tower has a large circular base built on a large square atop a sheer cliff, and its beam sweeps the sea with a range of 21 miles. Two low buildings, once used to house the keepers and fuel, are located near the lighthouse and are now used as storehouses for the machinery. Cabo Mayor is state-owned and run by the Santander Harbor Authority. Inside the lighthouse there is a plaque donated by the Santander Department of Commerce, which says:

"This lighthouse was built with many torments

is a safe guide on uncertain coasts

useful on fair days

essential on stormy ones

and honorable on other calmer ones

Year 1838"

SKERRYVORE

LIGHTHOUSE

The rugged western coasts of England, Wales, Scotland and Ireland are exposed to the terrible Atlantic storms and their deep natural bays are surrounded by rocky reefs that are submerged at high tide. Shipping has always had to face the danger of these rocks and many vessels were wrecked on these routes. It was thus necessary to build lighthouses in the most exposed areas, often on these very rocks in the middle of the sea.

During the first half of the 19th century a perilous reef off Scotland's northwestern coast, about 11 miles southwest of the Isle of Tiree in the Inner Hebrides, was chosen as the site for the construction of a lighthouse. The challenging feat was entrusted to the eminent Scottish maritime engineer Alan Stevenson (1807-1865). Stevenson belonged to what was to become an authentic dynasty of lighthouse builders. Indeed, his family built over 80 in the space of three generations. Alan himself built 12 and also became famous for having perfected Fresnel's lenses.

In June 1838 Alan Stevenson and his workmen landed on the rock known as Skerryvore, from Gaelic *Sgeir Mhor* ("mh" is pronounced as "v") meaning "great rock," to build the wooden barracks that would house the men during the construction of the lighthouse. Work could only proceed during the summer, because any kind of activity on Skerryvore during the winter was absolutely inconceivable. The men worked hard whenever the conditions of the sea allowed, and left the island in September. During the winter the barracks were swept away by a terrible storm. Although work in such conditions seemed impossible, Stevenson refused to be beaten and returned to the rock in spring 1839. New barracks were built and the foundations of the lighthouse were excavated using explosives. Work proceeded slowly and in terribly harsh conditions, for the sea continuously swept the surface of the rock and each time the men had to start again. However, the first part of the construction had been completed by the end of the summer. While the men were busy on Skerryvore, others were employed on the Isle of Mull quarrying the granite required for the tower. The blocks of granite were then dispatched to Tiree, where they were they were dressed so that each block fitted perfectly with the next, before being shipped in installments to Skerryvore. The workers returned to the rock on April 30, 1840, and the first stone was laid on July 4th. Work proceeded more rapidly that summer, and the workmen

67 ■ **The perfectly fitting stone blocks of Skerryvore Lighthouse have resisted wind and wave for over 160 years. Though raging seas frequently batter the tower's base, they have never damaged the structure .**

LOCATION	COORDINATES	HEIGHT	RANGE	CONSTRUCTION
SOUTHWEST OF THE ISLE OF TIREE, SCOTLAND	56° 19' N 07°06' W	157 FEET	26 MILES	1844

managed to lay as many as 85 blocks of granite. By the end of the season the tower had reached a height of over 7 feet. On May 20th 1841 work recommenced and a further 37 blocks were laid. In May 1842 the final part of the structural work was commenced and the last stone was laid on the top of the 136-foot tower in July of the same year. The construction of the lighthouse had required almost 4,750 tons of granite and the work of 150 men. In 1843 Alan Stevenson was appointed Engineer to the Northern Lighthouse Commissioners and entrusted the completion of Skerryvore to his younger brother Thomas, who fitted the interior of the lighthouse with 11 rooms during the same summer. The lantern was first lit on February 1st 1844, 6 years after work had commenced. The lighthouse has a tapered form and measures 42 feet across at the base, while the rooms on the top floor have a diameter of just 12 feet. However, it was neither comfortable nor convenient, for the keepers had to use ladders to pass between floors. Today the lantern is reached by a staircase of 151 steps.

The tower was damaged by fire on March 16th 1954 and a lightship served to provide the missing signal during the restoration, which lasted from 1956 to 1959 The lighthouse was electrified at the end of the 1950s, when three diesel generators were installed, and its beam of white light with a range of 26 miles has swept the sea at 10-second intervals ever since. A fuel storage house and a heliport were built near the lighthouse in 1972, to aid landing for the maintenance of the lighthouse, which was automated in 1994

Skerryvore Lighthouse is one of the most handsome 19th-century works of engineering and has been defined by the Institute of Civil Engineers as *"The finest combination of mass with elegance to be met within architectural or engineering structures."*

68-69 ■ A reef, a small rock and furious waves provided the setting for a 19th-century feat of engineering that would be difficult to achieve even today, using all the latest equipment.

CAPE
ST. VICENT
LIGHTHOUSE

[ALGARVE ■ PORTUGAL]

70 ■ The square inner courtyard of the lighthouse is surrounded by white colonnades, making it resemble the cloister of a monastery. The complex is dominated by the imposing and unusual red lantern.

70-71 ■ Cape St. Vincent Lighthouse watches over the breathtaking series of deserted rocky promontories that reach out into the Atlantic Ocean from Portugal's southeastern coast.

The last corner of Portugal to be glimpsed by sailors leaving their country thrusts out into the Atlantic Ocean from the southwestern end of the Algarve (from Arabic *al gharb*, meaning "Western Garden"). This rocky spur forms a large triangular headland known as Sagres Point that ends in Cape St. Vincent, a nerve center for ships sailing between the Mediterranean, via the Strait of Gibraltar, and Northern Europe and the Americas. This headland also played a strategic role in centuries past, before the advent of steamers, when the difficulty of handling great sailing ships against the wind made it necessary to descend down the Portuguese coast as far as Cape St. Vincent in order to find favorable winds that would carry them toward the Americas. In this region the rugged, rocky coast of the north gives way to a gentler landscape, characterized by a succession of sandy white beaches that reach as far as the Spanish border.

In remote times a group of Franciscan monks built a shelter for passing pilgrims on the tip of the headland, and in 1515 a small monastery surrounded by fortifications was erected on the site. The monks kept a fire burning here to show ships the way. The location of

72 ■ The interior of the lantern displays the amplification system installed at the beginning of the 19th century to maximize the beam's range.

↑

this corner of Portugal did not allow it to enjoy a peaceful history. In 1587 the "Queen's pirate," Sir Francis Drake, reached the Iberian coast and, after having attacked Cadiz, sailed northward, destroying several small fortresses, including the Fortaleza dc Beliche near Cape St. Vincent.

Despite the Algarve's turbulent history, the monastery expanded cnd in 1846 the engineer Parreira da Silva built a unique 82-foot (289 feet above sea level) round white tower on its roof, topping it with an enormous red-painted lantern measuring 13 feet high and over 4 feet across. Hyper-radiant Fresnel lenses with a range of 32 miles were installed in 1906, making the Cape St. Vincent Lighthouse one of the most powerful in the world. The signal was automated in 1982 and powerful white flashes have continued to shine out into the darkness ever since, keeping watch over the passing ships.

Location	Coordinates	Height	Range	Construction
Algarve, Portugal	37° 01' N 08° 59' W	82 feet (289 feet above sea level)	32 miles	1846

72-73 ■ There is nothing more evocative than the light of a lighthouse at sunset, when the sky is still rose-tinted and illuminated by the last ray of sunlight, before the burning lantern manages to cut through the darkness.

73 top ■ The outer courtyard of one of the low buildings that encircle the lighthouse is paved with stone and surrounded by a balustrade overlooking the ocean.

GIBB'S HILL

LIGHTHOUSE

[BERMUDA]

74 ■ The imposing white metal structure of the Gibb's Hill Lighthouse stands out against an almost tropical blue sky. The black metal wind vane at its base contrasts with the whiteness of the tower, dotted with many small square windows.

75 ■ Bermuda is a fairly flat island, but this little hill represented the ideal site for the construction of a lighthouse. The 115-foot tower is topped by a distinctive lantern surmounted by the radar antenna.

The Bermuda archipelago, which was discovered in 1503 by Spanish navigator Juan Bermudez, is composed of 150 islands, located in the Atlantic Ocean, in the Sargasso Sea, about 570 miles east of Cape Hatteras. The islands remained uninhabited until they became an English colony in 1684. Today only 20 islands are inhabited and linked by bridges. Great Bermuda, is 13 miles long and is the biggest island. Bermuda, Puerto Rico and the Florida Peninsula form a triangle, which was named after the archipelago and has sadly become famous as a "cemetery" for ships and planes. In fact, the Bermudas are the northernmost coral islands in the Atlantic, and the breathtaking reef that surrounds them has long represented a great hazard for sailors. The reef stretches over 16 miles along the western edge of the archipelago, and in the decade before Gibb's Hill Lighthouse was built, there were 39 shipwrecks in that part of the sea. As a result, the local authorities decided to build a lighthouse at the southwest of Hamilton. When the work began, no steel was available in the islands. Consequently, Gibb's Hill Lighthouse is one of the oldest conical lighthouses in the world to be made of cast iron. The structure was completed and tested on May 1, 1846. Designed to aid nav-

→ →

Location	Coordinates	Height	Range	Construction
GREAT BERMUDA, BERMUDA ARCHIPELAGO	32° 15' N 64° 50' W	115 FEET	25 MILES	1846

76-77 ■ As is a common practice, a metal grille surrounding the lenses of Gibb's Hill Lighthouse. From this height, the houses and ships on the sea look like part of a model land-and seascape.

igation, the lighthouse was built near the hurricane station, and in 1987 a radar transmitter was installed on top of the lighthouse to warn ships sailing too close to the barrier reef. The first lantern on Gibb's Hill was equipped with a lamp with four circular wicks. In 1904 it was replaced with a five-wick lamp, whose range was increased by the installation of Fresnel lenses. This lamp was used until 1923, when a kerosene-vapor burner was installed. The burner was maintained until the lighthouse was electrified in 1952, after which it was used until 1964 as a reserve unit in the event of power outages. Today, the lamp is powered by a 1000-watt bulb set in the middle of the lenses that were installed in 1904. For years, the movement of the lenses was driven by a clockwork mechanism with a weight that gradually dropped, thereby turning the lens. The mechanism had to be wound by hand every half hour. On June 4, 1964 the old mechanism was replaced with new electrical equipment. As noted in the Introduction, the large, heavy lenses that are installed in lighthouses to amplify their lighting power have always presented problems in terms of balance and rota-

tion. In about 1820, French physicist Augustin Fresnel invented a method that made it possible to sustain the weight of the thick glass lenses. He floated them in a bath of liquid mercury, thus ensuring smooth and continuous rotation. This ingenious invention revolutionized the construction of lanterns. However, the seas of Bermuda are often struck by hurricanes. One in particular, Hurricane Fabian, hit the tower so hard that the mercury overflowed from its bed, seriously damaging the base of the lenses. Urgent repair work was required and the contracting firm decided it was best to replace the old mercury system, which was not only dangerous for the structure but also toxic, with a system using a mechanical track. Gibb's Hill Lighthouse was reopened to the public one month after the hurricane, but in the meantime the decision was made to restore it completely. Therefore, electric bulbs that simultaneously send the same signal were installed on the four sides of the lantern while awaiting the replacement of the lenses. When it comes to trivia, there is a particularly interesting anecdote about the lighthouse. Several years ago, the granddaughter of the last lighthouse keeper bought the guardian's house and opened a tearoom there. Thus, the charm of this old structure has been enhanced by the opportunity for a refreshing break after climbing the 185 steps to the top of the tower.

Although Spain is considered a Mediterranean country, its northern and western coasts actually face onto the Atlantic. Unlike Britain, Spain has no lighthouses built on rocks in the middle of the sea because there are no reefs along its coast. The sea is deep almost all the way up to the shoreline and in certain spots even large ships can safely approach the coast. This explains why the setting and the actual architecture of Spanish lighthouses are far less dramatic than those of the Eddystone Lighthouse, for example, which rises out of the sea almost as if it were floating on its surface to mark the presence of fatal rocks. Spanish lighthouses are thus chiefly built to signal the presence of promontories that reach out into the sea and the entrances to ports. Castro Urdiales is an old seagoing city in the Cantabrian region on Spain's northern coast, 38 miles from Santander and 18 from Bilbao. Its very name Castro (*castrum*), evokes the ancient Romans, and following a remote past characterized by alternating fortunes, the city once again flourished after securing the traffic engaged in trade with the overseas colonies in the wake of the early voyages of discovery to America. Its population was decimated by the plague in the 16th century and its center was partially razed to the ground during the Napoleonic Invasion, but the city always managed to recover. Today its economy is booming, with mining, fishing and fish-canning industries and – most importantly of all – a healthy tourist trade. Castro Urdiales, like all ports, needed a lighthouse and the search for a suitable site in such a limited area led to its construction in an unusual position: the southeastern tower of the Castle of Santa Ana, a medieval building that is thought to have belonged to the Knight Templars. The keeper's house was built on the roof of the castle and the old chapel was used to house the machinery and as a maintenance workshop. The Castro Urdiales Lighthouse is a conical

CASTRO URDIALES

LIGHTHOUSE

[CANTABRIA ■ SPAIN]

←

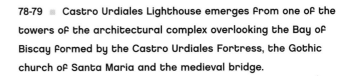

78-79 ■ Castro Urdiales Lighthouse emerges from one of the towers of the architectural complex overlooking the Bay of Biscay formed by the Castro Urdiales Fortress, the Gothic church of Santa Maria and the medieval bridge.

LOCATION	COORDINATES	HEIGHT	RANGE	CONSTRUCTION
CANTABRIA REGION – SPAIN	43°23" N 3°12" W	65 FEET	20 MILES	1853

stone tower, tapering slightly toward the top, surmounted by a tall bronze lantern, with an overall height of 65 feet. It is built on one of the five towers of the fortress, raising the lantern 160 feet above sea level. It was first activated on November 19, 1853, when its beam had a range of just 13 miles. The tower could only be reached by the castle stairs, while another staircase inside the lighthouse led up to the lantern. Behind the lighthouse is the Church of Santa Maria, a building in pure Gothic style. This particular stretch of the Spanish coast is very rainy and often enveloped in thick fog. In bad weather the light of the Castro Urdiales Lighthouse is all that can be seen through the grey blanket. The lantern was originally fueled by olive oil, which was later replaced by kerosene, before being supplanted by a 1000-watt electric lamp on February 8, 1919. Up until then the revolving motion of the lantern had been driven by a clockwork mechanism, which was replaced in 1926 by a floating system on a mercury bed. Other important changes were made during the same year: a six-foot diameter lantern with a mahogany interior was installed and the old stone steps leading up to the lantern were replaced with a metal staircase. A foghorn was added in 1953 and during the 1980s the flat-lens lantern was replaced with a curved-lens one with a range of 20 miles. The lighthouse has been considered an "architectural insult" to the castle. Nonetheless, in the collective imagery the city has become associated with its port, the Gothic Church of Santa Maria and the lighthouse on top of the castle. The objections of "purists" have, however, resulted in the creation of a separate entrance for the lighthouse and the removal of the machinery from the old chapel in order to restore the dignity of the castle, now a museum. The lighthouse is now state-owned and run by the Santander Harbor Authority.

POINT LOMA

LIGHTHOUSES

[CALIFORNIA ▪ UNITED STATES]

The San Diego coast, on the Pacific Ocean, is home to two lighthouses with the same name that are situated very close to each other, yet have completely different histories. The first, Old Point Loma, was built in 1854 and was one of the first eight lighthouses to be constructed along the West Coast. However its lantern was not it until November 15, 1855. This delay was due to the time required for the arrival from France of its third-order Fresnel lenses. The lighthouse was built on a site 420 feet above sea level, and its beam swept a wide area of ocean, reaching 25 miles. It was modeled on the New England lighthouses of the East Coast, which were built high above the imposing rocky coasts. However, on the Pacific coast the light was only visible in perfect weather conditions, because low clouds and fog banks often hid the lighthouse, making it ineffective. It nonetheless remained operational for 36 years, up until March 23,

80 ▪ The metal frame supporting the tower detracts from the appearance of modern-looking New Point Loma Lighthouse, built at the end of the 19th century.

81 ▪ The elegant metal pagoda roof of the lantern of Old Point Loma is decorated with a frieze that makes the structure appear lighter. The French-manufactured Fresnel lenses can be seen inside.

82 ■ The lenses of Old Point Loma Lighthouse, viewed from below, resemble a metal sculpture in a glass dome, reaching towards the blue sky.

1891, when it was deactivated and replaced by another built by the sea at the foot of the hill. The structure is comprised of a white sandstone keeper's house built in what is known as the "Cape Cod" style, topped by a 46-foot conical tower supporting a green-painted iron lantern. After long years of neglect, in 1913 it was decided to transform the lighthouse into a monument to the Spanish explorer and navigator Juan Rodriguez Cabrillo, who landed in San Diego Bay in 1542, becoming the first European to set foot on the West Coast of the United States. The lighthouse's new life commenced with the foundation of the Cabrillo National Monument, which in 1933 became the responsibility of the National Park Service and was placed on the National Register of Historic Places. Careful restoration work and the retrieval of much of the lighthouse's original furniture has enabled it to recover its original appearance and turned it into a tourist attraction. The lantern is lit each evening, although its range has been greatly reduced to avoid confusing approaching ships. The lighthouse is open to the public once a year on November 15th, to commemorate the day of its inauguration. The only time that it has been closed down was during the Second World War, when it was painted green and used as a landmark by the ships of the US Navy. Its signaling duties have been taken over by a new lighthouse, built at the foot of the hill and known as New Point Loma. The 69-foot white concrete tower is surrounded by a metal frame and topped by a black-painted lantern. It is flanked by the houses of the keeper and his assistants: a couple of two-story Victorian buildings that are now occupied by the Coast Guard and were recently used as the set for several scenes of the movie *Top Gun*. The Fresnel lenses once housed in the lantern were commissioned from the French firm Henri La Paute and were to have the same specifications as those of the old lighthouse. However, the manufacturer was so proud of his work that he presented the lenses at an exhibition in Paris, and

83 top The kitchen and living room of Old Point Loma faithfully reproduce the style of the period in which the lighthouse was built, making it seem as though it were still inhabited.

successively at the Chicago Columbian Exhibition. Because of this delay, other lenses were installed in the lighthouse and used for the first time on March 23, 1891, when the old Point Loma light was extinguished. The original lenses from France ended up in the Chicago Harbor Lighthouse. The New Point Loma Lighthouse is currently operational and is not open to the public. Access to visitors is restricted to the surrounding area, which is an excellent spot for sighting the gray whales whose annual winter migration route brings them close to the coast.

82-83 ■ The white bulk of Old Point Loma Lighthouse, with its lantern lit, stands out against the rose-tinged sky as sunset. Although the lighthouse is no longer used, it continues to occupy its original site and is open to the public.

LOCATION	COORDINATES	HEIGHT	RANGE	CONSTRUCTION
SAN DIEGO, CALIFORNIA, UNITED STATES	32° 43' N 117° 11' W	46 METRI	25 MILES	1854

BISHOP ROCK

LIGHTHOUSE

[CORNWALL ■ GREAT BRITAIN]

Britain is renowned for its open-sea lighthouses, the most famous of which is undoubtedly Eddystone, south of Plymouth. These signal towers are essential because of the country's rugged coastline and outlying rocky reefs, which are often submerged at high tide and exposed to the terrible force of the Atlantic storms. This is an extremely dangerous combination of factors for shipping. West of the Scilly Isles, lying off the Cornish coast, countless rocks rise from the seabed to graze the surface of the water. One in particular—Bishop Rock—became sadly famous when the British frigate *H.M.S. Romney*, armed with 50 guns, was wrecked and sank along with her entire crew of 400 men. The small lighthouse that had stood on the island of St. Agnes since 1680 was not sufficient to cover all of the surrounding area, and so Trinity House, the general lighthouse authority for England, Wales, the Channel Islands and Gibraltar, decided to build one on Bishop Rock itself. The islet is just 150 feet long and 52

84 ■ The original plans for the lighthouse were drawn up by James Douglass in 1867. The drawing on the left shows a cross-section of the tower with the supporting base, while that on the right illustrates the extra story planned for the existing lighthouse.

85 ■ The circular base keeps the Bishop Rock Lighthouse stable. A helipad allows for inspection of the lighthouse.

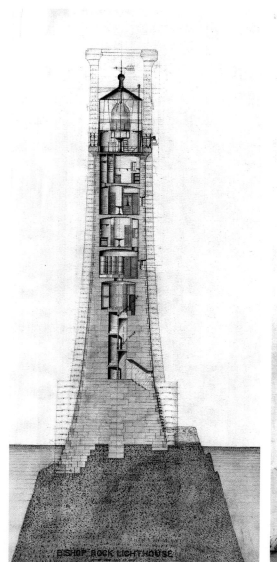

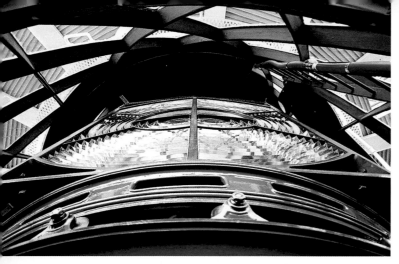

Location	Coordinates	Height	Range	Construction
Cornwall, Great Britain	49° 52' N 6° 26' W	144 feet	24 miles	1858

feet wide, and it was thus quite a challenge to construct anything on it. Indeed, even Trinity House's Engineer-in-Chief, James Walker, commissioned to build the lighthouse, initially opposed the plan to build a stone tower on such a small rock that was exposed to the full fury of the sea (experiencing over 30 gales a year, according to his own estimate), where it was unlikely to withstand the strong winds. Work began in 1847, when £12,500 was appropriated for a project featuring the construction of a cast-iron lighthouse. The large tubular structure was to be anchored to the rock by six cast-iron piles, for the designer maintained that the waves would be able to roll freely among them instead of being obstructed by a solid mass of masonry. The 118-foot tower was completed in 1849, except for the lantern, which was to be installed at a later stage. However, on the night of February 5, 1850, the entire structure was swept away by an incredibly strong gale, which also caused damage on the Isles of Scilly.

James Walker, who was working under the supervision of Nicholas Douglass and his son James, was undismayed and decided that the second Bishop Rock Lighthouse would have to be built using the technique employed by Smeaton for the Eddystone Lighthouse. He found a relatively flat portion of rock, where he built the base for the lighthouse. However, this area was always covered with water, and so a cofferdam was built around the site and the seawater constantly pumped out in order to allow the masons to work on a dry rock face. It was grueling, difficult and slow work. The granite blocks, each weighing one or two tons, were dressed and assembled on the mainland, fitted into each other to form a solid mass, and then numbered and shipped to the islet, where they were reassembled in the correct position. The 115-foot lighthouse required 2,755 tons of granite, took seven years to complete, and cost £34,560. The lantern was lit on September 1, 1858 and Prince Albert praised the work as a triumph of technology and tenaciousness. Unfortunately this tower did not last long either. Soon after its inauguration a huge wave tore away the fog bell 98 feet above the ground, and on April 20, 1874 the tower was pounded by waves at least 115 feet high, which caused it to shake dangerously, making the keepers fear for their safety. Indeed, the structure was found to be unstable: the movements of the tower caused the lens prisms to break and the foundations also started to subside. In 1881 Sir James Douglass drew up a revolutionary plan of work to reinforce the building, encasing it in a new lighthouse that was not only stronger, but also 39 feet taller. On May 25, 1883 his son William commenced work, strengthening the foundations by build-

ing a tall granite retaining wall around the base, which was sunk into the rock and anchored to it by strong bolts. The old lighthouse continued to function as work proceeded on the new tower. Ropes were used to lay the new blocks of granite, as it was impossible to construct scaffolding. Upon completion the lighthouse weighed 6,305 tons, was 144 feet tall and had cost £66,000. The third Bishop Rock Lighthouse was inaugurated on October 25, 1887. The lighthouse was electrified in 1973 and automated in 1991. The last resident keeper departed in 1992. A helipad has now been installed above the lantern to allow the landing of technicians for periodic maintenance.

86-87 ■ English and Scottish engineers were the first to dare to build lighthouses on small rocks in the middle of the sea. The secret of their success was due to their solid structure and tapered shape: for design calculations revealed that the vertical mass and weight were sufficient to withstand the assault of the waves.

LOCATION	COORDINATES	HEIGHT	RANGE	CONSTRUCTION
PROVINCE OF TRAPANI, SICILY, ITALY	38° 11' N 12° 44' E	131 FEET	18 MILES	1859

SAN VITO LO CAPO

LIGHTHOUSE

[TRAPANI, SICILY ■ ITALY]

Sicily, ancient Trinacria, is the largest Mediterranean island and lies off the southwestern coast of Italy. It has seen the passage of many peoples and civilizations (Greeks, Arabs, Normans and Bourbons), each of which has left their mark on the island: Greek theaters, Saracen fortresses, magnificent Norman cathedrals and sumptuous Bourbon palaces. The Bourbons, who ruled the island for over a century, were the indirect champions of several lighthouses, built during the very last years of their reign. One of the best-known lighthouses is that of San Vito Lo Capo, a small town built on a flat area on the northern coast of the island, 20 feet above sea level, and about 25 miles from Trapani.

The spot was pinpointed in 1854 as the ideal site for the construction of a coastal tower. Work commenced immediately and was completed five years later. The lighthouse was inaugurated and the lantern lit for the first time on August 1, 1859. The cylindrical tower was 131 feet tall and built on top of a single-story block that housed its keepers. The entire building was painted white. In 1860, just a few months after it was built, Sicily was annexed to the Kingdom of Italy and the lighthouse became the property of the Royal Civil Engineers. An official document drawn up by the King's technicians in 1873 contains an accurate description of the structure.

The lighthouse was originally equipped with a vegetable oil lamp, which was replaced in 1887 with three-burner kerosene lamp, with a range of 18 miles. The building at the base of the lighthouse was extended during the same year and in 1919 an incandescent lamp fueled by vaporized kerosene was installed. In 1910 all lighthouses became the responsibility of the Royal Navy's Lighthouse Service and in 1936 the interior of the tower was modernized, the old machinery replaced with more up-to-date equipment and the power of the lantern increased. The lighthouse was finally electrified in 1938 and equipped with a 1,000-watt bulb. The old kerosene-vapor lamp was relegated to the role of emergency light, but the lantern had to wait until 1964 before it was fitted with a 1,000-watt/120-volt halogen bulb. The lighthouse is still operational today: its lamp emits a white flash every 5 seconds and still has its original range of 18 miles.

89 ■ The elegance of the white tower of San Vito, seen from below, is clearly visible in its small windows with pale surrounds and its Neoclassical-style cornice. The lantern's beam has illuminated the Sicilian sea for over a century.

CRÉAC'H
LIGHTHOUSES

[OUESSANT ISLAND, BRITTANY ■ FRANCE]

Although in the past France was backward in respect to the rest of Europe in terms of lighthouse building, its coasts are now some of the best lit and monitored of the entire continent. During the late 19th-century drive to construct lighthouses, the French adopted the strategy of building a sequence of them so that ships could sight the light of one as soon as they had left behind that of another. Thousands of lanterns are installed along the French coasts, and 120 of these are located along Brittany's Finestère Peninsula, the first stretch of land to be sighted by ships arriving from America. The northwestern tip of this peninsula is home to the most powerful lighthouse in Europe, which is also the most important due to its strategic function for maritime traffic between the English Channel and the Atlantic. It is situated on a rock that rises high out of the ocean and is known as the Créac'h (meaning "rise" in Breton) or Ouessant Lighthouse.

The imposing 130-foot tower was built in 1863 to protect the area's increased shipping, which was also due to the development of overseas colonies. The island was already home to the old Le Stiff Lighthouse, which was built in 1695 and only lit during the winter. However it was

90 ■ The photograph shows an unusual, calm winter landscape. The black and white banded tower with its tall lantern rises above the square of snow-clad buildings that surround it.

91 ■ Créac'h Lighthouse is set in a Dantesque landscape, amidst houses, rocky pinnacles, the stormy ocean and fog caused by the ocean spray. Only the mild sunlight reduces the drama of the scene.

92 and 93 top ■ Elegant wooden paneled interiors are not unusual in French lighthouses. The wood warms the atmosphere and the ceiling is decorated with a wind rose. The entrance hall, with its spiral staircase, is also completely clad with wooden panels.

just 105 feet tall and not sufficient to prevent shipwrecks on the rugged coast; its light was not bright enough. The rise upon which Créac'h Lighthouse was built is situated opposite a stretch of razor-sharp jagged rocks, pounded by the full force of the ocean waves. It has been calculated that at the beginning of the 20th century least 30,000 ships passed close to Ouessant Island, which is often shrouded in fog – the main cause of accidents in the area.

Like all lighthouses, Créac'h has been subject to numerous modifications. In 1888 it was electrified and equipped with a new and more powerful optical system. It was modernized in several stages over the following 40 years, with three different optical units that doubled the range of its beam to 34 miles. A foghorn was also essential and a modern siren was installed in 1900. It was replaced with a bell in 1912, which was supplanted in turn by a vibrating system located on the terrace of the lighthouse in 1985. In 1987 the lantern was even equipped with a signaling system to prevent it from being hit by migrating birds in flight.

The lighthouse uses a xenon bulb with a life of 5,000 hours. The keepers have to wear protective gloves and masks when replacing it. Xenon (whose name is derived from the Greek word xenos, meaning "strange") is an inert, odorless and colorless noble gas that was discov-

Location	Coordinates	Height	Range	Construction
Ouessant Island, Northern Finistère, France	48° 27' N 5° 07' W	180 feet	34 miles	1863

ered by William Ramsey and Morris W. Travers in 1898, and became used in arc lamps and flash and fluorescent bulbs. When a charge of electricity is passed through xenon it produces an explosion of bright white light. This system makes the two white flashes emitted by Créac'h Lighthouse every ten seconds the most powerful in Europe.

In 1988 the old electrical power station at the foot of the lighthouse was converted into the Musée des Phares et Balises, a museum housing the finest collection of Fresnel lenses in the whole of Europe, including those of Le Cordouan, along with exhibits recounting the history and development of lighthouses.

The Créac'h Lighthouse has a cylindrical tower with black

92-93 ■ Though the ocean's fury assails Ouessant Island, the lighthouse towers unscathed above the waves.

and white bands and is topped by an iron lantern. Its base is surrounded by a semicircular arrangement of buildings. Its simple, linear outer appearance contrasts strongly with its interiors: the walls are entirely paneled and inlaid with wood and the ceiling at the top of the spiral staircase is decorated with a wind rose made from different-colored woods. The result is a luxurious, warm atmosphere, resembling an English gentleman's club. The French love of beauty has even found its way inside a lighthouse, a building that our stereotypes envisage as the very epitome of bareness and austerity.

The nearby Le Stiff, Nividic, La Jument, Kéréon and Pierres Noires Lighthouses are all monitored and controlled from Créac'h Lighthouse.

94-95 ■ The powerful white flashes of Créac'h Lighthouse cut through the night, lighting the jagged rocks at its foot. The beam of light is indeed salvation for sailors.

95 bottom ■ The powerful Fresnel lenses housed in the lighthouse's lantern are surrounded by glass windows covered with a metal lattice for protection from the fury of the elements.

96 ■ The elegant
lantern of Chipiona
Lighthouse evokes
Moorish architectural
features: its shape is
more reminiscent of
the terrace of a
minaret than that of
a lighthouse.

CHIPIONA

LIGHTHOUSE

[ANDALUSIA ■ SPAIN]

96-97 ■ Chipiona is one of the handsomest and most
elegant lighthouses in Spain. Its tower rises above a
square building to overlook the Gulf of Cadiz.

Chipiona Lighthouse, at the mouth of the Guadalquivir River (or Betis, as the Romans called it) in Andalusia, was designed by the architect Eduardo Saavedra and built on the ruins of a preexistent Roman lighthouse. Its light first illuminated the Andalusian coastal waters on November 28, 1867. At 207 feet (226 feet above sea level), it is the tallest lighthouse in Spain and one of the tallest in Europe. The Guadalquivir is Spain's only navigable river and Seville has been one of the country's most important trading ports since Roman times, when the mouth of the river was already the site of a lighthouse called Turris Caepionis, built by the general Quintus Servilius Caepio.

Following the discovery of the New World, Seville, the Guadalquivir and, above all, Cadiz became strategic for trade with the American colonies.

In 1762 a lighthouse was designed to mark the entrance to the river, but it was never built. In 1855 there was talk of building a 328-foot tower on the Salmedina rocks, however this overly ambitious idea was abandoned due to its high cost. The current lighthouse was designed in 1862 by Saavedra. The 180-foot tower has a 46-foot base and several outbuildings to house the keeper and store the fuel. The lighthouse was built in 1867 and equipped with an olive oil burning lantern with clockwork mechanism, with a range of 23 miles.

The monumental external appearance of Chipiona Lighthouse is matched by the elegance of its interior. An arched doorway leads into the square base housing a courtyard, which resembles the entrance to a noble residence rather than a lighthouse, surrounded by two stories of arches and topped by a glass pyramid that admits the light and keeps out the bad weather. It is embellished by iron lamps hanging from the arches and green plants around the edges. On one side a spiral fretted iron staircase with 344 steps leads up to the lantern, which houses the splendid Fresnel lenses. The entire building is made from stone and the tower, with four windows, culminates in an overhanging cornice that supports a terrace edged by elegant iron railings. The structure is topped by the imposing lantern. This lighthouse is not only an example of the great Spanish public works of the 19th centu-

ry, but also is a great artistic achievement.

The lighting system has been modified over the years: the first lantern was fueled by olive oil, its revolving movement was driven by a clockwork mechanism and it flashed a white light followed by an eclipse at one-minute intervals. In 1916 the lighting system was replaced by a lamp with 3_-inch burners fueled by pressurized and vaporized kerosene and the rotation of the lantern was increased to allow a flash-eclipse period of 15 seconds. In 1925 a fixed light was installed that signaled a sequence of three white flashes plus one. The lighthouse was electrified in 1942, when the kerosene lamp was replaced with a 300-watt bulb. However, the lantern underwent its most drastic transformation in 1964, when the old clockwork mechanism was removed

Location	Coordinates	Height	Range	Construction
Andalusia, Spain	36° 45' N 6° 26' W	207 feet	25 miglia	1867

and replaced with a modern rotation unit and an air-sea type of lighting system was installed that emits a white beam with a range of 25 miles every 10 seconds. On days with good visibility, its light can be seen as far away as the Portuguese coast.

The old lighting system and the clockwork mechanism removed in 1964 are housed in the warehouses of the Seville Harbor Authority. The lighthouse has a resident keeper, and the entire building is open to the public.

Roman civilization was already "modern" in its own way, for its sailors knew that there was no endless abyss waiting to swallow up ships beyond the Pillars of Hercules. Consequently, the Romans reached the coasts of the Iberian peninsula, France and England, and wherever they built a port, they also constructed a lighthouse. Many of these disappeared long ago, destroyed by time and harsh weather conditions, apart from that of La Coruña, whose base is Roman, and Turris Caepionis, which lives on in the Chipiona Lighthouse like a monument recalling the ancient civilization.

98-99 ■ Each day the keeper of Chipiona Lighthouse climbs the spiral staircase that leads to the lantern to carry out the maintenance and cleaning of the lenses and the entire structure.

PEGGY'S COVE

LIGHTHOUSE

[NOVA SCOTIA ■ CANADA]

Though Peggy's Cove Lighthouse is one of the best-known and most photographed in the world, little is known about its history. Its official name is "Peggy's Point Lighthouse" and it is in Nova Scotia, Canada, on the east coast of Saint Margaret's Bay. The little fishing village of Peggy's Cove, with a population of about 60 people, is located nearby.

All lighthouses are fascinating, but some spark the imagination more than others: though it is not imposing in size, Peggy's Cove Lighthouse is one of these. Set at the end of a low promontory of granitic rock that formed immediately after the Ice Age, it stands proudly with its octagonal white shape and unmistakable red lantern. Many versions and legends are tied to its name: Peggy is a nickname for Margaret and many say that it was named after Saint Margaret's Bay. According to the most credible legend, however, Peggy was the name of the sole survivor of a shipwreck that occurred nearby, though the year is unknown.

Documents demonstrate that in 1868 a wooden lighthouse was initially built on the roof of the guardian's house, with a lantern that emitted a red light and a round mirrored reflector to increase the range of the kerosene lamp up to 10 miles. Following Canada's turn-of-the-century policy of expanding and consolidating its lighthouses, in 1915 a new octagonal cement tower was built a few yards west of the original one. The new lighthouse emitted a white light whose range was increased by dioptric lenses composed of a set of glass prisms. The old tower, which was no longer used, was nevertheless left in place for many years, until Hurricane Edna destroyed it in 1954.

The new lighthouse is 50 feet tall (65.5 feet above sea level) and is very stark. The year 1969 marked its most dramatic change, when its white metal lantern was painted red. Since 1979 its lamp has emitted a steady green light with a range of 13 miles. The lighthouse also boasts another unique feature. Since 1972 its ground floor has also housed a post office, which is only open during the summer. Anyone can send a letter or postcard from this unique post office – and its stamp will have a decidedly original postmark.

101 ■ **Peggy's Cove Lighthouse stands on a huge granite rock worn smooth by the elements and the centuries. Its red lantern has stood sentinel over the Atlantic Ocean since 1954.**

 102-103 ■ The tower and the rocks below, which date back to the
Ice Age, are white with the snow of the cold Canadian winter.

103 bottom ■ The two-colored outline of the lighthouse
stands out against the night sky. Although the tower is not
very tall, its solitary location makes it visible for many miles.

LOCATION	COORDINATES	HEIGHT	RANGE	CONSTRUCTION
SAINT MARGARET'S BAY, NOVA SCOTIA, CANADA	ì44° 29' N 64° 6' O	15 METRI	13 MIGLIA	1868

CAPE
HATTERAS

LIGHTHOUSE

[NORTH CAROLINA ■ UNITED STATES]

The Cape Hatteras Lighthouse is probably one of the best known and most widely photographed in the United States. President Thomas Jefferson commissioned construction of the first lighthouse on the site, completed in 1803, from the architect Henry Dearborn, who subsequently became his Secretary of War. The tower has a very distinctive silhouette, with a red-brick and granite platform and black and white spiral stripes. At 197 feet, it is the highest brick lighthouse in the United States. Its beam has a range of approximately 20 miles and illuminates the waters off the Outer Banks, at Buxton, North Carolina. The Outer Banks are a sandy barrier that runs parallel to the coast. One sandbank in particular, known as the Diamond Shoals, is considered the most dangerous area of the Outer Banks. The ideal site was pinpointed in 1789 on atop a small hill on Cape Hatteras and, following various delays, the construction of the original building, entrusted to Henry Dearborn, was completed in 1803. The 89-foot tower featured a 10-foot lantern lit by 18 whale-oil lamps, but this light was not bright enough to be seen at a safe distance by ships. In 1815 the 18 whale-oil lamps were replaced with a system of Argand lamps patented by Winslow Lewis. However, even

104 ■ This view from below shows the distinctive black and white spiral pattern of Cape Hatteras Lighthouse. Tall tapering lighthouses are typical of low sandy coasts.

105 ■ A US Coast Guard aircraft over Cape Hatteras; the photograph was taken in 1996, when the lighthouse was still in its previous location, already dangerously close to the seashore.

this was not powerful enough to light these dangerous waters. Nonetheless, it was not until 1852 that the necessary funds were appropriated for radical improvement work. The tower was raised to a height of 148 feet and the lantern equipped with Fresnel lenses. Cape Hatteras survived the devastation of the Civil War, but by the end of the conflict, in 1865, it was decided not to repair it because of the high cost. In March 1867 the United States Congress appropriated funds for the construction of a new tower. The lighthouse, completed in 1870, was 197 feet tall and has survived to the present day substantially unchanged. The lighthouse's main enemy over the years has been erosion by the sea. It was feared that the lighthouse could be destroyed by the fury of the ocean, and so a new tower was built on a small wooded hill about a mile and a quarter west of the existing one. This 148-foot metal framework tower was completed in 1936. However, the ocean is strange and unpredictable, and started receding during the same period. By 1937 it had returned to a distance of almost 650 feet from the base of the tower.

In 1942, during the Second World War, the Cape Hatteras Lighthouse was decommissioned once again and became a sighting tower for German U-boats. At the end of the War the Park Service and the Coast Guard jointly planned major renovation work on the old tower. Now that the ocean was at a safe distance, it was decided to reactivate the Cape Hatteras Lighthouse – which had been electrified in 1934 – to substitute the new metal framework tower. Work was completed in 1950, and the newly restored lighthouse commenced duty with an efficient revolving optical unit. Another more powerful optical unit was installed in 1972. During the 1990s engineering experts from the University of North Carolina decided that the lighthouse would have to be relocated. This feat– which seemed impossible to many – was completed on September 14, 1999, just before Hurricane Dennis swept the coast of North Carolina. The keepers' houses were moved first of all, followed by the tower, which was relocated half a mile southwest of its original position. The Cape Hatteras Lighthouse is now situated approximately 550 yards from the sea. The tower reopened to the public on May 26, 2000.

106 and 107 ■ This sequence shows Cape Hatteras Lighthouse in its original position, during the relocation process and, finally, in its new setting at a safe distance from the erosive effects of the sea. Cape Hatteras Lighthouse is now open to the public during the summer. Those willing to tackle the long climb up to the top of the tower can enjoy a view over the Outer Banks from the terrace around the lantern.

LOCATION	COORDINATES	HEIGHT	RANGE	CONSTRUCTION
BUXTON, NORTH CAROLINA, UNITED STATES	35° 13' N 75° 32' W	197 FEET	20 MILES	1870 (RENOVATED 1950)

BODIE ISLAND
LIGHTHOUSE

[NORTH CAROLINA ■ UNITED STATES]

A sandy barrier known as the Outer Banks runs along the coast of North Carolina, from southern Virginia to South Carolina. This barrier is not continuous and the inlets between the sandbanks allow the internal waters to mingle with those of the Atlantic Ocean. The long tongue of sand also reaches out into the sea for several miles, creating treacherous and constantly moving sandbanks, which are very dangerous for shipping. Two currents meet in this area of sea (the warm Gulf Stream and the cold Labrador Stream), constituting a further peril to passing ships. It is no coincidence that the area in front of the Outer Banks is known as "The Graveyard of the Atlantic."

The need to build signal towers on this stretch of coast resulted in the construction of tall lighthouses situated as close as possible to the sea. In 1837 the federal government sent a naval officer, Napoleon Coste, to inspect the area in order to find the most suitable site for the construction of a lighthouse. The officer pinpointed Bodie Island, slightly north of Cape Hatteras.

Congress approved the plan in 1803, but construction was delayed due to the difficulty of purchasing the required land, and the lighthouse was only built in 1847. The project had been entrusted to the experienced engineer Francis Gibbons; but during construction allowance was not made for the characteristics of the sandy terrain and the 52-foot tower started to lean almost immediately. Despite a series of reinforcement operations, the lighthouse had to be abandoned in 1859. Another tower, 79 feet tall and equipped with Fresnel lenses, was built nearby during the same year and immediately proved itself to be far more solid than the first one. Like Cape Hatteras, Bodie Island was also caught up in the vortex of the Civil War. The Outer Banks were occupied by Union troops in 1861 and Confederate forces destroyed the lighthouse during their retreat to avoid it being used by the enemy. At the end of the conflict, the Outer Banks remained unlit for several years. The Lighthouse Board, which was the body then responsible for the building and maintenance of the coastal signal system, only commenced the construction of a new lighthouse in 1871. The tower was located slightly further north than the previous one and its site was purchased by the government from a certain John Etheridge for the sum of $150. Work proceeded slowly, sharing some of the materials used for the

109 ■ **Bodie Island Lighthouse is the third to have been built in this spot. The previous two towers were erected slightly south of the current site, but succumbed to the inaccessibility of the area and the Civil War.**

contemporaneous building of the Cape Hatteras Lighthouse. Finally, on October 1, 1872, the lantern of the third Bodie Island Lighthouse was inaugurated. The tower was 154 feet tall and equipped with magnificent Fresnel lenses, which gave it a range of 19 miles.

During the months immediately following the inauguration a house was built for the keeper and his family. However, the isolation of the lighthouse and the difficulty involved in transport and supplies called for its urgent electrification and semi-automation. These changes were made in 1932, making the presence of a permanent keeper unnecessary.

In 1953 the land surrounding the lighthouse was transferred to the National Park Service, which was already responsible for the territory of Cape Hatteras. However, the structure itself continued to be run by the Coast Guard until July 14 2000, when it too was taken over by the National Park Service.

Bodie Island Lighthouse is still operational and is not open to the public. The two-story wooden keeper's house has been converted into a visitors' center and houses the Park Ranger's office and a small museum documenting the

Location	Coordinates	Height	Range	Construction
Bodie Island, Outer Banks, North Carolina, United States	35°57' N 75°37' W	154 feet	19 miles	1872

building's long history and misfortunes. However the conditions of the structure are critical. The American *Lighthouse Digest* magazine has published a list of lighthouses in danger for many years now, and that of Bodie Island has been featured on it since the beginning of 2000. The lighthouse has recently been restored externally, but the iron lantern clearly shows the ravages of time, the outer rail is being consumed by rust, and the precious first-order Fresnel lenses are awaiting repair. The National Park Service has drawn up a renovation plan designed to restore the lighthouse to its original splendor over the next few years.

110-111 ■ The lighthouse's spiral fretted iron staircase has a unique feature: it is not perfectly round like others of its kind, because its steps are interrupted by a small semicircular balcony at each floor.

111 ■ A foggy night makes the light of Bodie Island Lighthouse even more evocative. Although this is perhaps one of the lesser-known lighthouses of the Outer Banks, it is just as important as the others.

LONGSHIPS
LIGHTHOUSE

[CORNWALL ■ GREAT BRITAIN]

The Scilly Isles are located off the southwest coast of England. The southernmost island, St. Agnes, was already the site of a lighthouse as early as 1680. However, its signals were not sufficient to warn of the perils of this highly dangerous area. Indeed, the islands are surrounded by a reef of rocks, which extends toward the coast of the mainland and is often submerged by the high tide, becoming a deadly trap for vessels heading both northwest and south of Great Britain.

Europe's Atlantic coast was one of the first to be equipped with signaling towers, constituting a great advantage for trade, which benefited from increased shipping safety, but also a considerable source of profit for the associations and communities that ran the lighthouses and collected considerable transit duties. Consequently, over the years, eight large lighthouses were built on a stretch of coast no longer than 50 miles.

Longships Rock, whose highest point reaches 140 feet above the sea at high tide, belongs to the dangerous and notorious Scilly Rocks. It is situated 1.25 miles off Land's End, making it the ideal site for a lighthouse. The first 36-foot tower was privately built in 1795 by Captain Henry Smith, to whom it was rented by Trinity House for a 50-year period. However, for some unknown reason, its management was soon transferred to the British authority. The lighthouse was equipped with an oil lamp that emitted a fixed light and continued to be used for 75 years. However, its signal was not strong enough and the sea often submerged the lantern, as its position was too low. Trinity House thus decided to build a taller and stronger tower on the same rock. Around 1870, the engineer William Douglass (1831-1923), of the famous dynasty of lighthouse builders, was commissioned to design the new tower. Longships II was completed in 1875. Five years were required to overcome the numerous difficulties encountered on the isolated rock, including the high tide, which limited working time to a few hours a day. The problems to be solved included the construction of the base of the tower, which had to be built by manpower, with the help of heavy equipment that was difficult to transport. The blocks of stone for the tower were hewn one by one on the mainland and shaped to fit each perfectly, before being loaded onto special craft fitted

113 ■ Longships Lighthouse was the second to be built on this rock off the Cornish coast, surrounded by a low reef that is often submerged by the high tide.

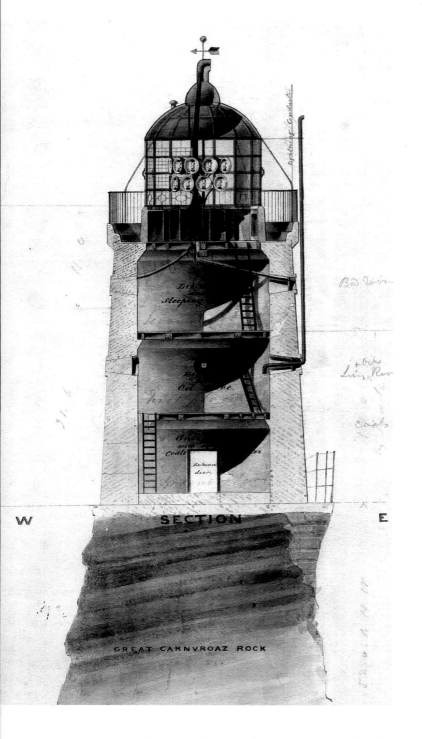

114 ■ The original plans for the first
Longships Lighthouse date back to around
1792. This section shows sketches of the three
internal floors of the tower. The picture of
the lantern shows the original lamps with
reflecting mirrors.

115 ■ Many British open-sea lighthouses are
surmounted by a small helipad. This has made
it possible to eliminate the presence of
keepers in such isolated areas. The structure
of the lighthouse is one of the narrowest of
its kind, and the keeper's quarters were
decidedly uncomfortable.

with rollers, which were used to move the blocks, and transported to the rock, where they were unloaded by cranes, ready for use. Lighthouses built on rock must have a low center of gravity and their height must not be greater than three and a half times the diameter of their base in order to ensure their stability.

Upon completion, Longships Lighthouse measured 115 feet and was topped by a lantern equipped with a vaporized kerosene lamp with a range of 18 miles that emitted a white flash followed by a red one at five-second intervals. The tower had to be very slender in order to satisfy the rules of construction and the diameter of the round rooms was less than 8.5 feet, including the space for the stairs leading to the lantern. Life on Longships Rock could not have been easy. Similarly, the rotation of the lighthouse keepers was no simple matter, due to both the isolated position of the rock and the conditions of the sea, which often made it inaccessible. The employment contract required that half the men be collected once a month and the other half every two months. The changeover represented quite a feat: a boat approached the rock and the keeper about to commence duty was raised by a crane operated by the men inside the lighthouse and the same system was used for those leaving. The provisions were then hoisted up and finally the crane was once again stowed away inside the lighthouse to protect it from the stormy sea. As there were no refrigerators, the provisions consisted of dry or salted foods. All these difficulties led the authorities to request and obtain the automation of Longships Lighthouse, which ceased to be manned by a keeper as far back as 1967.

Seen from the sea, immediately after Bishop Rock when sailing toward Liverpool, Longships Lighthouse has an imposing appearance: a dark tower with small windows along the upper section and a terrace around the lantern featuring a framework surmounted by a large circular platform for the landing of the small helicopters used for the periodic inspections of the maintenance technicians.

LOCATION	COORDINATES	HEIGHT	RANGE	CONSTRUCTION
CORNWALL, GREAT BRITAIN	50° 04' N 05° 44' W	115 FEET	18 MILES	1875 (FIRST LIGHTHOUSE IN 1795)

BROTHERS ISLANDS
LIGHTHOUSE

[RED SEA ■ EGYPT]

Egypt evokes the memory of history's first great lighthouse: the Lighthouse of Alexandria, built around 300 B.C. on the island of Pharos facing the city and recognized as one of the Seven Wonders of the World. The two tiny El Akhawain islands – better known as Brothers Islands – are situated about 37 miles off the Egyptian coast, southeast of Hurghada, where the Eastern Desert meets the Red Sea. The islands are two coral plateaus standing no more than 33 feet above sea level, which rise out of an abyss about 1,650 feet deep. Shipping in this area of sea became very intense following the opening of the Suez Canal, as attested by the numerous wrecks that lie on the seabed. The Red Sea was the shortest route used by the British to reach their colonies in India, and indeed it was the Crown – whose possessions then also included part of the eastern coast of Egypt – that decided to build a signal network to improve the safety of shipping in the 1880s.

A lighthouse was thus constructed on Big Brother Island, using the practically free labor of Egyptian prisoners. The 118-foot tower was completed in 1882. The kerosene lamp was fueled by a manual pump that had to be activated every four hours and its light was intensified by Fresnel lenses that gave it a range of 17 miles. The optical system, manufactured by Chance Brothers of Birmingham, weighed over a ton and was operated by means of a complex system of counterweights that were raised and lowered inside the tower. The lighthouse was inhabited by the chief keeper and four assistants, who had the task of lighting it at sunset, fueling

it every four hours, and extinguishing it at dawn. The life of the keepers was uncomfortable to say the least: they had no electricity, their sole means of contact with the mainland was represented by an old battery-powered Morse transmitter; supplies were rare, landing on the island was difficult and fishing was their only means of subsistence. The men worked shifts of three months on the island and one at home, or nine months on the island and three on the mainland.

The lighthouse was electrified and automated in 1994, when the old lens was replaced by a lamp with a range of 17 miles that emits 4 white flashes every 16 seconds. Since the departure of the keepers, their old houses made of local stone — the only testimony of an age of astounding feats and sacrifices – have been falling into ruin.

116 ■ The lighthouse that stands on the coral plateau of Big Brother Island, just above the surface of the Red Sea, towers over the old keepers' houses that are now abandoned.

116-117 ■ The lighthouse was automated in 1994 and its powerful lenses, capable of producing a beam with a range of 17 miles, are controlled from the mainland. The solitude of the building is interrupted only by periodic inspections and maintenance visits.

LOCATION	COORDINATES	HEIGHT	RANGE	CONSTRUCTION
RED SEA, EGYPT	23° 39' N 36° 09' E	118 FEET	17 MILES	1882

EDDYSTONE
LIGHTHOUSE

[DEVON ■ GREAT BRITAIN]

England has a long seafaring tradition, which is perhaps the reason behind the first lighthouses built along the country's coasts. These took the form of light signals, which warned ships of shallows and rocks. Eddystone, on the southern coast of England, about 13 miles south of Plymouth, is one of the most famous English lighthouses and also one of the oldest in the world. It was erected on the rock of the same name, sadly notorious for its countless shipwrecks, and has a tormented history, for it was rebuilt four times.

Trinity House, the body responsible for the maritime signaling system along the English coast, started to examine the project as early as 1664, but construction of the lighthouse was only commenced 30 years later, in 1696, with the appearance of Henry Winstanley, an eccentric ship owner and inventor. Winstanley had lost two of his ships on the rock and accepted the challeng of building the lighthouse, obtaining authorization from Trinity House to collect the profits from transit duties for five years.

Construction was fraught with difficulties, and it was only possible to work on the rock when the sea was calm. During construction of the lighthouse Winstanley was captured by a French privateer and carried off to France, then at war with England. A legend tells that King Louis XIV imprisoned the pirate in the Bastille and freed Winstanley with the following words, "We are at war with England, not with humanity." Actually, it appears that Winstanley was exchanged for several French prisoners in England. The inventor recommenced work and the lighthouse was completed toward the end of 1698. The 79-foot wooden tower with stone base was inaugurated on November 14, 1698. However, winter in the Atlantic can be very hard and the lighthouse was already in need of urgent repair by the following spring. Its fanciful architect not only reinforced the base with metal rings and raised the lantern to a height of 118 feet, but also improved the comfort of the tower by adding a decorated bedroom, a veranda and a living room with open gallery. The renovated building was inaugurated in October 1699.

Winstanley was so confident of the structure that he declared that he would like to be in the lighthouse during the most violent storm ever. His wish

119 ■ **The Eddystone Lighthouse has been rebuilt four times. The tower shown in the photograph is the last of the series, erected in 1882. The base that can be seen alongside is what remains of the third lighthouse, which was dismantled in 1870.**

was tragically fulfilled a few years later, on November 27, 1703, when he visited it for a routine inspection and spent the night there. The following morning the lighthouse had disappeared, swallowed up by the sea along with its builder and all those who were in it, during one of the most terrifying storms ever to have hit the English coast.

Rebuilding was commenced several years later and the task was entrusted to John Rudyerd, who obtained a license allowing him to collect transit duties from passing ships for 99 years. This former silk merchant based his design on shipbuilding principles. The 69-foot conical wooden structure was inaugurated in 1709 and stood for 47 years,

outliving its builder. However, on December 2, 1755, a terrible fire broke out on top of the lantern, which was lit by several dozen candles. The chief keeper and two assistants tried in vain to put it out by throwing water upward from a bucket.

By this time the lighthouse had become essential to shipping, and was thus rebuilt yet again. The undertaking was assigned to John Smeaton, a civil engineer, expert in mills and precision instruments, and the inventor of Portland cement (a material very similar to quick-setting cement that is still used today), which he employed in the construction of the lighthouse. The new stone tower was built on the mainland and subsequently reassembled block by block. It was inaugurated in October 1759 and remained in use for 120 years, until cracks were noticed in the rock upon which it stood. Fear of collapse led to it being dismantled in 1870 and rebuilt on dry land, at Plymouth Hoe, according to the wishes of the city's inhabitants, who financed the relocation.

However, Eddystone did not remain without a lighthouse. As the rock was no longer sound and the relatively advanced technologies of the time enabled the construction of underwater bases, Sir James Douglass, a Trinity House

engineer used a cofferdam to build the foundations of the new all-granite tower beneath sea level. It was inaugurated in 1882, near the stump of the structure that was dismantled and reassembled in Plymouth.

The Eddystone Lighthouse is 161 feet tall and equipped with Fresnel lenses with a range of 22 miles. It emits two white flashes every ten seconds and can be recognized by a distinctive feature that it shares with some other English lighthouses: its glass dome is topped by a frame that supports a helipad. The lighthouse is still in use today. It was electrified long ago and automated in 1982.

120 ■ The lantern's beautiful Fresnel lenses amplify its light.

120-121 ■ Seen from above, the lighthouse almost appears to be flattened against the sea. It is topped by a helipad for the transport of the technicians responsible for its periodic maintenance.

LOCATION	COORDINATES	HEIGHT	RANGE	CONSTRUCTION
DEVON, GREAT BRITAIN, 13 MILES SOUTH OF PLYMOUTH	50°10'80'' N 04°15'90'' W	161 FEET	22 MILES	1882 (PREVIOUS BUILDINGS: 1698-1699-1709-1759)

MACQUARIE

LIGHTHOUSE

[NEW SOUTH WALES ■ AUSTRALIA]

Toward the end of the 18th century Australia, which was then an almost unexplored land and destination of emigrants seeking their fortunes, became a sort of British penal colony. The transportation of prisoners to Australia also allowed the British crown to colonize an almost uninhabited territory. The names of the newly settled areas often paid tribute to the old country, such as New South Wales, in southeastern Australia. Control of this region was entrusted to naval officers up until 1810, when the experienced Scottish-born general Lachlan Macquarie (1761-1824) was appointed governor to replace William Bligh, the famous captain of the *Bounty*. He commenced a program of important public works, using the forced labor of the convicts and the services of Francis Greenway (1777-1837), an architect who had been exiled for political reasons and subsequently regained his freedom thanks to his work. In 1791 bonfires were lit on a rise on the southern side of the entrance to the port of Sydney — then known as Port Jackson — with the purpose of guiding the first ships arriving from England. It consisted of a simple wood-burning brazier, whose flame remained the sole signal on that point of

122 ■ **Macquarie Lighthouse stands on a high cliff that drops sheer to the sea below. The Australian Post Office commemorated the 150th anniversary of the construction of the first lighthouse on the Australian coast with the issue of a stamp.**

123 ■ **The elegant white lantern of the second lighthouse built on the site stands out against the blue southern sky. The lighthouse is a monument to a farsighted governor who had understood the potential of a frontier land like Australia in the early 19th century.**

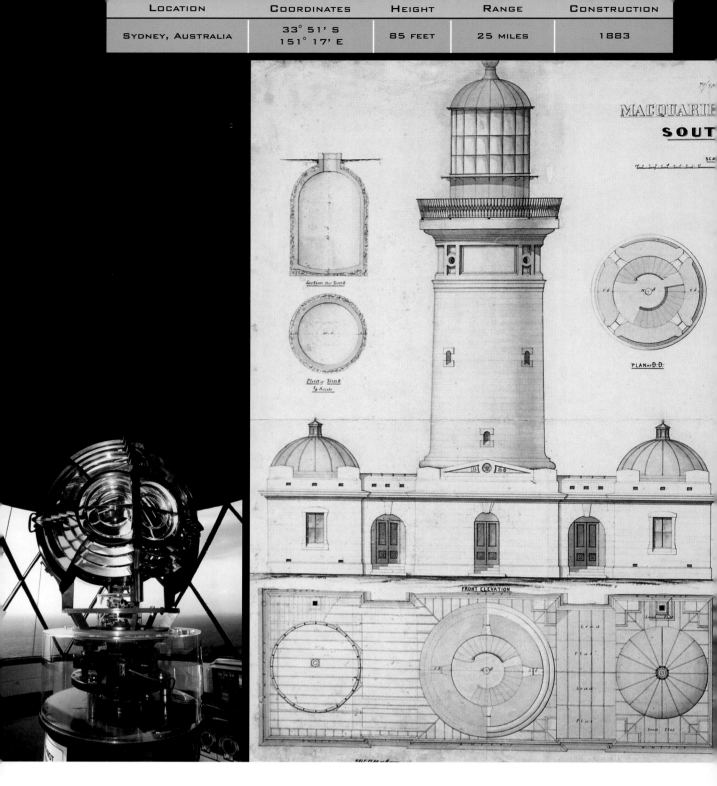

MACQUARIE

SOUT

PLAN at D.D.

FRONT ELEVATION

124 ■ The small, but powerful, British-manufactured lenses housed in the center of the lantern room are based on the system devised by the French physicist Augustin Fresnel.

124-125 ■ These are the plans for the construction of the second Macquarie Lighthouse, dated 1879. They show details of the lighthouse, base, cross-section and tower, and are housed in the National Archives of Australia in Canberra.

the coast for the following 25 years. The first sandstone lighthouse was commissioned by Governor Macquarie, after whom it was named, and designed by Greenway. The lantern was lit on November 30, 878 and featured a series of oil burners with a clockwork-driven revolving lens that emitted a white flash with a range of 22 miles every minute. However, the poor quality of the construction material resulted in the rapid deterioration of the tower. When the architect told the governor that the lighthouse would not last long, the tower was reinforced by placing iron bands around its base. However, in 1878 it was finally decided to build a new lighthouse. The task was entrusted to James Johnstone Barnet (1827-1904), a Scottish architect who emigrated to Sydney in 1854 and became official Colonial Architect in 1865. The new lighthouse was a copy of the first. However, it was built from stronger materials so that the top of the tower could support the lantern, which was larger than the previous one and surrounded by a bronze railing. This detail was also to become a distinctive mark of the other lighthouses subsequently built by the architect. The lantern housed an optical system manufactured by Chance Brothers of Birmingham and consisting of giant revolving

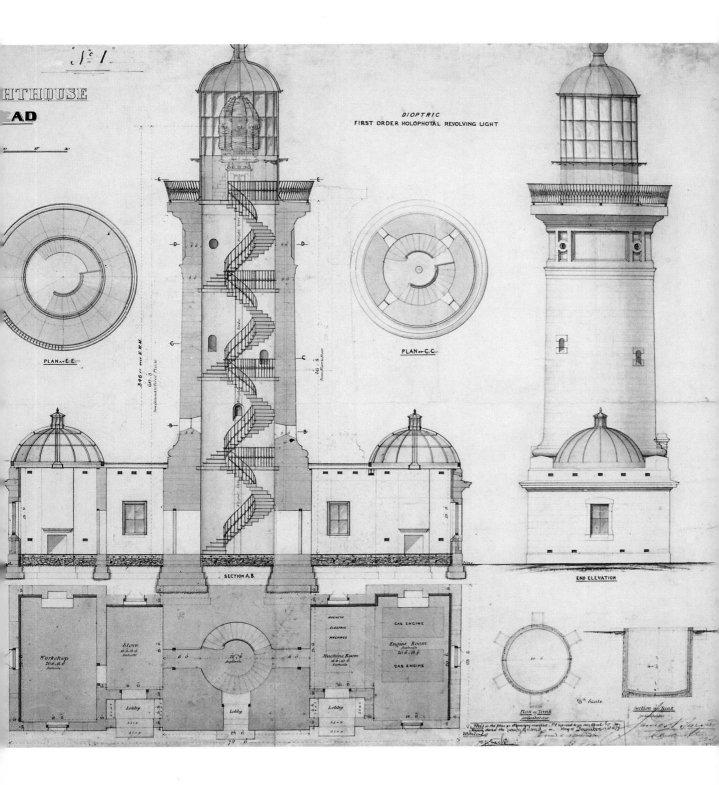

dioptric lenses based on the Fresnel system, with a diameter of about six and a half feet, which emitted a white beam with a range of 25 miles every minute. In adverse weather conditions the Port Jackson lighthouse functioned electrically by means of two De Meritens magnetos, which weighed 2.75 tons and were driven by an eight-horsepower coal-gas engine. One of these generators is now on display in the lighthouse's museum. In good weather the lantern was lit by a gas burner. The old building was not demolished immediately: the lantern was removed, but the tower was left standing for several more years. The old generator was too expensive to run so it was removed and replaced with a kerosene-vapor burner in 1912. The lantern was electrified in 1933 and a new system of smaller, but equally powerful, lenses was installed. The lighthouse was automated in 1976 and the last keeper left it in 1989. The architecture is characterized by a blend of colonial and Victorian styles and dominated by the color white. The base of the building is formed by a block with three arched entrances. The central one is surmounted by a pediment decorated with the New South Wales state emblem and a brightly painted bas-relief bust of Queen Victoria with the royal insignia. The roof features two vaguely oriental-style domes on either side of the mighty cylindrical tower, which is topped with the lantern resting on a small terrace surrounded by iron railings.

HECETA HEAD

LIGHTHOUSE

[OREGON ■ UNITED STATES]

Heceta Head is a rocky spur on the northwestern coastline of the United States, near Florence, Oregon. It owes its name to Don Bruno de Heceta, a Spanish explorer who sailed northward along this stretch of coast in 1775, on a secret mission for the Spanish crown. This rocky bluff was the most northerly point that he managed to reach before being forced to turn back in order to treat his men, who were suffering from scurvy. In 1862 the spot was officially named Heceta Head.

The Spanish captain had already noted on his maps that the sea in this area was dangerously shallow and dotted with jagged rocks that broke its surface, but it was not until the mid-19th century that the local authorities decided to build a lighthouse here. Up until then there had been little maritime traffic in the area, but the situation changed as droves of pioneers headed west. New cities were founded along the coast and existing ones expanded. The ports were enlarged and shipping became more intense, with sometimes disastrous consequences. In 1888 the site was chosen for the construction of a lighthouse that would sup-

126 ■ The first American lighthouses on the West Coast of the United States were modeled on those of the East Coast. Passing ships paid great attention to these lighthouses built atop high slopes.

127 ■ The white tower of Heceta Head Lighthouse contrasts with the brown rocks. The small white house next to it was long the home of the keeper and his family.

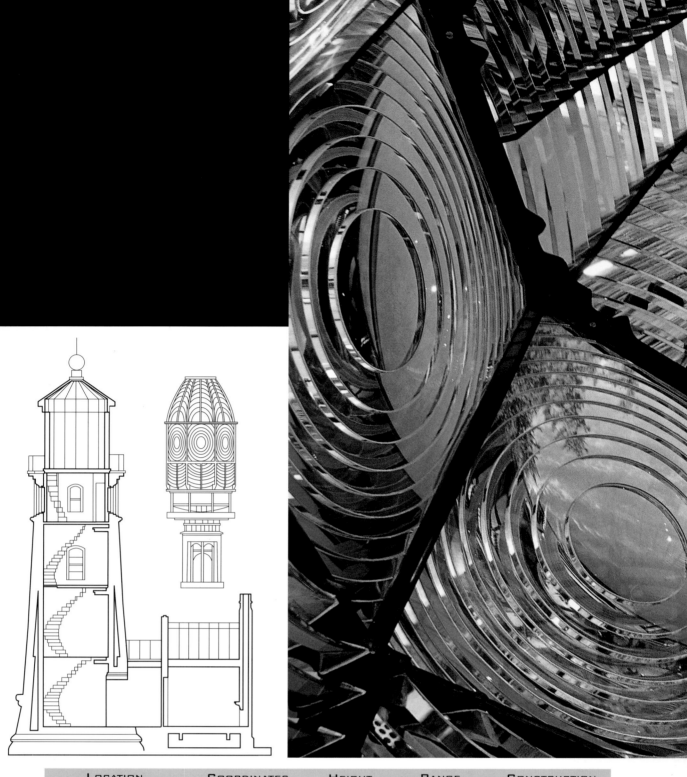

Location	Coordinates	Height	Range	Construction
FLORENCE, OREGON, UNITED STATES	44° 1' N 124° 8' W	56 FEET	21 MILES	1894

128 ■ This late 19th-century drawing shows a cutaway view of the lighthouse and the lantern, the lower floor and the beautiful Fresnel lenses still in the equip.

128-129 ■ A play of lights inside the glass dome enclosing the lighthouse's lenses provides the backdrop for the two electric bulbs that illuminate the Pacific Ocean each night.

plement those of Cape Arago and Yaquina Head. Building commenced around 1890 and difficulties were immediately encountered, as the rock towered almost 165 feet above sea level in a very isolated location. The Lighthouse Board engineers had to resort to complex expedients to build the tower: the base could only be created by the use of explosives and part of the construction materials had to be transported by sea, unloaded along the Suislaw River and carried up to the rock by mules. Two years and great expense were necessary to complete the lighthouse, oil storage cistern, cabin housing the foghorn and two Queen Anne-style wooden houses – a single-story one for the chief lighthouse keeper and a two-story one for his two assistants. On March 30, 1894 the five-wick oil lamp was finally lit by the chief keeper Andrew Hàld, displaying the full splendor of its first-order Fresnel lenses, manufactured in England, whose light was and still is visible for 21 miles.

The lighthouse is built in the colonial Spanish Revival style and con-

sists of a small white building with a red roof flanking a 56-foot conical brick tower. The tower is surmounted by a green-painted iron lantern 203 feet above sea level, surrounded by a small terrace allowing for maintenance of the glass from the outside.

Life cannot have been easy for the keepers of the isolated Heceta Head Lighthouse, and indeed it is said that the early ones did not stay there long. An exception was Olaf Hansen, who remained from 1896 to 1920, except for a brief two-year interval between 1902 and 1904. This eclectic personality not only looked after the lighthouse, but also ran a little post office and, when a small school was built in the neighborhood in 1916, even acted as teacher.

However, all this changed following the completion of the Oregon Coast Highway between Florence and Yachats in 1932. The highway passed close to Heceta Head, finally connecting the remote spot to the surrounding area. The lighthouse was electrified in 1934 and the old lighting system was replaced with a new one with bulbs. It was also decided that fewer keepers were now necessary, and the second assistant was dismissed. The chief keeper went to live in the two-story house and the other was demolished.

In 1963 the lighthouse was automated and its last keeper, Oswald Allik, was also dismissed. The Coast Guard continued to maintain the lantern, but

130-131 ■ The oval Fresnel lenses shine out from Heceta Head's lantern in the foggy twilight. This lighthouse is considered the most powerful of the entire Oregon coast.

the rest of the complex fell into disrepair. In 1970 the keeper's house threatened to collapse, making urgent restoration work necessary. A group known as the Friends of Heceta House was founded for this purpose. The building was leased to Lane Community College, which used it to house class-rooms and for student accommodation while restoring it. In 1978 Heceta Head Lighthouse was placed on the National Reg-ister of Historic Places, thus assuring the ongoing mainte-nance of the entire complex. The lighthouse is now part of the Heceta Head State Park and the keeper's house is a private-ly run bed and breakfast inn renowned for its gourmet breakfasts.

The light of the powerful lantern can be seen at a distance of 21 miles from Heceta Head.

CAPE BYRON
LIGHTHOUSE

[NEW SOUTH WALES ■ AUSTRALIA]

The pretty little seaside resort of Byron Bay is situated in New South Wales, on the eastern coast of Australia, about 500 miles north of Sydney and 110 miles south of Brisbane. On the easternmost side of the town is a small promontory called Cape Byron, an ideal spot for the construction of a lighthouse. It is said that Captain Cook named the area Cape Byron, after John Byron, the grandfather of the famous English poet. A lighthouse made from blocks of reinforced concrete was inaugurated here on December 1, 1901. It was designed by Charles Harding following the style of James Barnet, who had been official colonial architect and designer of the Macquarie Lighthouse, which the Cape Byron Lighthouse resembles. The first-order lenses installed in the lantern weigh almost nine tons and are composed of 760 pieces of prismatic glass. They were manufactured by the Henry Lepante company of Paris and were moved by a clockwork mechanism. The concentric six-wick burner had a lighting power of 145 candles. In 1922 this system was replaced by a kerosene-vapor burner with 500 candlepower. When the Cape Byron Lighthouse was electrified in 1956, it became the most powerful in Australia, at 2,200 watts, and the clockwork mechanism was replaced by an electric motor. A subsidiary red light was subsequently installed to signal two dangerous rocks to the northeast. A great banquet was prepared to celebrate the inauguration of the lighthouse and all the leading personalities of the day were invited, including the NSW Premier, John See. However, the ship transporting the important guest was delayed by bad weather and stormy seas. Despite this setback, the opening celebrations were still held, and others were arranged when Mr See finally arrived. Macquarie Lighthouse, Australia's oldest, and Cape Byron Lighthouse, its most powerful, are very similar in structure. Both consist of a white block topped with a tall, solid tower culminating in a great lantern above a terrace with metal railings. In the case of Cape Byron, this last detail is a tribute by the architect, Charles Harding, to his famous predecessor James Barnet.

132-133 ■ Cape Byron Lighthouse is the most powerful in Australia and stands on the easternmost promontory of the entire continent. This spot was long wild and isolated, but is now a popular tourist destination.

Location	Coordinates	Height	Range	Construction
New South Wales, Australia	28° 38' S 153° 38' E	59 feet (387 feet above sea level)	27 miles	1901

ÎLE VIERGE

LIGHTHOUSE

[NORTHERN FINISTÈRE ■ BRITTANY, FRANCE]

Île Vierge is a small island off the northwestern coast of France, in the region known as Finistère (from Latin *Finis Terrae*, meaning "end of the earth"), which is tragically well known to sailors due to its dangerous jagged coasts. The island itself is merely the largest of a low reef of rocks strewn across the sea, which represents a constant danger, especially at high tide. The French government purchased the island in 1840 to build a lighthouse on it. The 105-foot square granite tower – with a range of 14 miles – was inaugurated on August 1, 1845, but it immediately became clear that it was inadequate to light the wide area of sea.

In 1882 the authorities decided to build a new lighthouse without demolishing the old one, but work only commenced in 1897. However, the results, upon completion in 1902, were magnificent: the cylindrical, 269-foot, dark Kersanton granite tower with a 43-foot base was the tallest in Europe, exceeding even that of Genoa, which – at 252 feet – had until then held the title. It is necessary to climb 365 steps to reach the top of the tower, plus an additional 35 up to the lantern, making a total of 400 steps. The entire wall surrounding the long spiral staircase is covered with 12,500 blue milk-glass tiles manufactured in Italy, which stretch right up to the ceiling, creating the impression of an aquarium. These tiles actually have a practical purpose, for milk glass is made from a mixture of powdered bone and glass that protects the walls from dust and dampness. The walls surrounding the stairs of an earlier French lighthouse, at Eckmühl, also feature the same type of decoration although in this case the tiles were manufactured by the French company Saint-Gobain.

The lighthouse was originally powered by kerosene, but was electrified in 1956. Energy is supplied by a wind-powered storage battery and the light is generated by a 650-watt halogen bulb, which emits a white flash every 5 seconds, and has a range of 27 miles. The foghorn, which sounds for three seconds every three minutes, has been installed in the old lighthouse, which also houses the keepers' quarters.

Although located on an islet less than a mile from the mainland, this lighthouse is considered an "open-sea lighthouse" to all intents and purposes. Tide permitting, the tower can be visited between June and September, when its keepers willingly accompany tourists up its long staircase to admire the magnificent view from the top of the lighthouse.

135 ■ The massive granite tower of the new Île Vierge Lighthouse rises above the old square lighthouse that is still intact. A very tall building, visible from a great distance, was required to add to the safety of this stretch of sea.

136 ■ Île Vierge boasts Europe's highest stone lighthouse. Visitors can pick up a brochure at the entrance that illustrates the history and building stages of the two lighthouses in great detail.

←

136-137 ■ Those wishing to tackle the 400-step climb can enjoy a spectacular view over the sea surrounding Île Vierge, which is protected by a jagged reef that is often submerged by the waves.

↑

Location	Coordinates	Height	Range	Construction
Northern Finistère, Brittany, France	48° 38' N 04° 34' W	269 feet	27 miles	1902

137 bottom ■ The surprising spiral staircase inside the lighthouse is entirely covered with blue milk-glass tiles, manufactured in Italy. They reflect the light, creating a pleasant atmosphere.

FASTNET ROCK

LIGHTHOUSE

[CORK ■ IRELAND]

Fastnet Rock is located about three and a half miles off the southwest coast of Ireland. This 85-foot tall rocky pinnacle in the middle of nowhere is surrounded by very strong currents and exposed to the full force of the perpetually rough sea. A legend tells that the rock was thrown into the middle of the sea by the devil, in order to obtain souls from shipwrecks. The number of ships wrecked in this part of the sea seems to bear the legend out. In 1818 there was already a lighthouse on the island of Cape Clear, but it was not very visible, due to the frequent presence of thick fog. In 1848, the year after the wreck of the *Stephen Whitney*, an American ship, in which 90 passengers perished, the authorities decided to build a lighthouse on Fastnet Rock. The task was entrusted to George Halpin who, like his father, had already built lighthouses all over Ireland and elsewhere in the United Kingdom.

The structure was made from cast iron, and great difficulties involved in its erection because of the terrible conditions of the site. The lantern was lit on January 1, 1854 with a powerful oil lamp, but it became clear almost immediately that the structure would not have with-

138 ■ Fastnet Lighthouse, photographed against the light, appears as a little dot in the middle of the ocean.

139 ■ The characteristic tapered tower stands upon an almost inaccessible rocky spur.

stood the severe weather conditions for long and that it was almost impossible for boats to moor for the changeover of staff and delivery of provisions. The men were forced to live shut up in the lighthouse in very difficult conditions for a month or more at a time. In 1868 the base of the structure was reinforced, but in 1881 the lantern was seriously damaged by a storm. Ten years later it was decided to build a new granite lighthouse on the western part of the rock, in a more protected position than the original site.

The new lighthouse was designed by William Douglass. Work commenced in 1899 and took five years to complete. It was a colossal undertaking: the blocks of Cornish granite (a total of 2,074 were used, with an overall weight of 4,740 tons) were shipped to Rock Island, from where they were transported to Fastnet Rock aboard the *Ierne*, a ship built specifically for the purpose. Each block of granite was dovetailed into those around it using a construction technique that resulted in an incredible tower that was a single, great stone monolith. The light-ing system was designed and manufac-

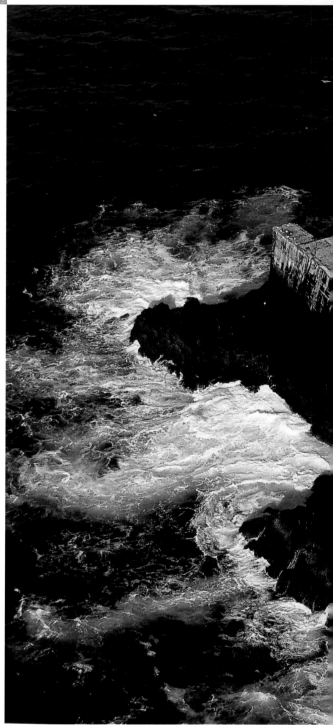

tured by Chance of Birmingham and featured a revolving mechanism that floated in a mercury bath and two kerosene burners. The cost was enormous at the time, topping £90,000. The lighthouse was inaugurated on June 24, 1904. The old cast-iron tower was dismantled down to the first floor and used as a fuel storehouse. It can still be seen close to the new lighthouse. On May 10, 1969 the old vaporized kerosene lamp was replaced with an electric one. The lighthouse is 177 feet tall, falling to 161 feet at high tide, and its white beam, which flashes every 5 seconds, has a range of 27 miles. In 1974 the lighthouse was equipped with an electric fog signal — an essen-tial feature in these waters — that sounds four times each minute. It has a range

141 top ■ The lenses housed in the lantern were manufactured in England, but were built using the same principle as Fresnel's lenses, refracting the light of the electric bulb and directing it towards the center.

→

Location	Coordinates	Height	Range	Construction
County Cork, Southwest coast of Ireland	51° 23' N 9° 36' W	177 feet	27 miles	1904

of 3.9 miles and replaced the old foghorn that had been installed in 1887. The lantern also remains lit when the fog signal is active during the day. Lighthouses are surrounded by an air of romance and adventure and fascinate all who see them. Fastnet Lighthouse is no exception. The imposing isolated structure in the middle of the sea appears to thrust its roots into the rock and the tower, dotted with little windows, culminates in two small terraces below the high dome that houses the

140-141 ■ Fastnet Lighthouse appears in its full majesty in this photograph taken from a helicopter. The automation of the lighthouse has required the addition of a helipad for the transport of the technicians responsible for its maintenance.

lantern. The lighthouse has been uninhabited since 1989, but is periodically visited by a technician who reaches the rock by helicopter to perform the necessary maintenance.

Fastnet Rock and its lighthouse are also famous for the annual boat race held in these waters, but few people know that in Ireland it is known as the "Teardrop" because it was the last corner of the country glimpsed by the Irish emigrants headed for America and the hope of a better life. Fastnet Lighthouse also marked the last land sighted by the passengers of the *Titanic*, the new, unsinkable transatlantic liner, as it steamed toward its tragic destiny.

142-143 ■ The light refracted by the Fresnel lenses transforms the dioptric prisms into a large tropical butterfly.

143 bottom ■ The sun sets behind Fastnet Lighthouse and shows the true solitary nature of the rock: a little corner of Ireland cast into the middle of the sea.

LA MARTRE
LIGHTHOUSE

[QUEBEC ■ CANADA]

Seen from the land, La Martre Lighthouse offers a picture-postcard view: a 36-foot octagonal wooden tower, painted bright red, near a small red building on a plateau that is white with snow in the winter and emerald green in the summer.

La Martre Lighthouse, also known as River Martin Light, is situated on the northern coast of the Gaspé Peninsula, on a small hill close to the village from which it takes its name. The French word martre means "marten," a very common mammal — along with whales and seals — on the southeastern coast of Canada, where the St. Lawrence River meets the Atlantic Ocean.

Canada is a huge country with over 150,000 miles of coast overlooking three oceans, four lakes and numerous navigable rivers. Its morphology requires an efficient network of lighthouses, capable of marking the most dangerous points of such an extensive coastal system. Consequently, at least 1,700 of the structures were built in the space of 250 years, along the coasts of the country's oceans and inland waters.

144 ■ The small red building close to the lighthouse houses a permanent exhibition detailing the history and development of lighthouses and their lanterns and their importance to shipping.

145 ■ La Martre is unique among lighthouses. Although it is not very tall, its octagonal shape and red color make it visible from a great distance even during the day.

In 1876 the first square tower was built at La Martre. It was made of white painted wood and
stood near the keeper's house. However, it rapidly deteriorated, perhaps
due to the harsh weather conditions or neglect, and the current lighthouse
was built in 1906. This too was made of wood, but it was octagonal in form
and the keeper's house was erected farther away. This lighthouse was also
initially painted white. However, no consideration had been given to the fact
that the structure was located on the broad St. Lawrence River's southern
bank, which is covered by ice and snow during the winter months, and that
the lighthouse's color made it barely visible. The structure was consequently repainted an unusual shade of barn red, with a vertical white stripe. However, this was subsequently changed and the tower assumed its present
solid red color. The octagonal tower is topped by a tall, round, cast-iron
lantern, which was also painted red. Two concentric terraces were placed
between the lighthouse and the lantern. The wider is used as a passage to
access the lantern; the narrower one immediately beneath the lantern is

used by the keeper to clean the glass from the out-side.

La Martre is the only lighthouse in the province of Quebec not to have been automated. Its lenses float in a mercury bath, while the lantern is turned by a clock-work movement driven by weights.

Though designed to aid navigation, La Martre Light-house has become a unique landmark on this stretch of Canadian coast. The red tower perfectly comple-ments the landscape, characterized by forests that slope down to the sea.

146-147 ■ Another attraction of the village, located near the lighthouse, is the little Sainte-Marthe Church, built in 1914. The exterior of the church is entirely finished in cedar shingles, unique in this area. The mouth of the St. Lawrence River, covered with a thick layer of ice and snow during the winter, can be seen in the background.

LOCATION	COORDINATES	HEIGHT	RANGE	CONSTRUCTION
GASPÉ PENINSULA, QUEBEC, CANADA	49° 12' N 66° 10' W	36 FEET (131 FEET ABOVE SEA LEVEL)	17 MILES	1906

TASMAN ISLAND

LIGHTHOUSE

[TASMANIA ■ AUSTRALIA]

The southeastern coast of Tasmania is jagged and ravished by terrible storms that sweep the islands scattered across Storm Bay. Tasman Island is a small rocky islet with sheer walls rising around 820 feet above the sea to a grassy plateau. The flat part was once thickly wooded, but is now bare as over time the lighthouse keepers felled all the trees for firewood.

The island is situated just over half a mile from Cape Pillar, on the tip of the Tasman Peninsula. This may be a short distance elsewhere, but not in this area of sea. In 1906 one of Australia's most isolated lighthouses was built on the highest point of the island, 905 feet above sea level. The 95-foot lighthouse consists of a round tower made from cast-iron plates that rests on an 85-foot diameter reinforced concrete base. The lantern featured a 3.5-inch vaporized kerosene burner and the lenses were manufactured by Chance Brothers of Birmingham and are now housed in the Australian National Maritime Museum. The keepers' cottages were built from brick, as were the coal and wood sheds, and shared a solid roof to protect them from the fierce winter storms.

The Tasman Island Lighthouse's history is closely linked to the human fortunes that have accompanied it for almost a century: the adventures and tragedies of an area of sea in which survival alone is a difficult task. A fairly rudimentary cableway was built to transport building materials onto the island; it was subsequently also used to transfer the keepers and their families and to deliver provisions. It consisted of a sort of basket hanging from a hook that was maneuvered from above, and was more of a precarious shell than an elevator. However, it was absolutely essential for survival and consequently was carefully maintained by the keepers. Indeed, so much attention was dedicated to keeping it in good order, that only one accident was documented during the lighthouse's long years of activity. It was also possible to reach the sea by a steep and narrow path that zigzagged its way down the cliff but it was so difficult to negotiate that it was used only in cases of dire need.

Tasman Island was undoubtedly an unpopular destination with the lighthouse keepers, for it was difficult even to deliver provisions to that scrap of land in the middle of nowhere, swept by violent winds. The only alternative source of food came from tending the small cultivable areas of land and raising cows and sheep, but the plateau was so dangerous that a fence was built

149 ■ **Tasman Island Lighthouse is one of the tallest in Australia and stands atop a breathtaking sheer cliff that falls into the wild waters of Storm Bay, 820 feet below.**

all around the lighthouse and the cottages to prevent children and livestock from falling off the cliffs. Communications were so difficult that the keepers used pigeons to send messages to the mainland.

Even the lighthouse itself had a hard life in such extreme conditions. Its lantern was damaged by wind during the very first year following its construction, as the keeper reported in his log on March 20, 1907: *"The tower vibrated to such an extent that it shook the mantles to pieces; had to substitute the wick-burner at 2 a.m."* In 1919 another terrible storm blew away the roofs of the cottages and the tower shook so much that the mercury spilled out of the bath in which the lenses floated and onto the floor. During construction the severity of the local weather conditions was underestimated and the windows of the lighthouse were fitted without waterproofing. The lantern room was frequently flooded as a result.

In 1933 a radio connection was finally established to Hobart, the Tasmanian capital, and two other nearby lighthouses, allowing for the immediate summoning of help and

150-151 ■ Tasman Island is a little rocky islet off the southeastern coast of Tasmania, which forms a kind of grassy plateau. It was once thickly wooded, but the lighthouse keepers cut down all the trees in their quest for firewood.

151 bottom ■ The modern and highly technological lighthouse is now completely automated. The helicopter shown in the photograph is used to transport the technicians responsible for the routine maintenance of the lighthouse.

Location	Coordinates	Height	Range	Construction
TASMAN ISLAND, SOUTHEASTERN TASMANIA	43° 14' S 148° 00' E	95 FEET	39 MILES	1906

the reception — and more frequently transmission — of meteorological information. Subsequently the island was connected by helicopter and life at the station became much easier.

The lighthouse was automated in 1976, when the dome was replaced in order to accommodate new and more powerful lenses. It was experimentally powered by a wind generator, but two diesel generators were also installed for back-up purposes. The following year the keepers abandoned the lighthouse for good. Finally, the wind generator was replaced by solar power in 1991.

SPLIT ROCK
LIGHTHOUSE

[LAKE SUPERIOR ■ MINNESOTA, UNITED STATES]

The North American Great Lakes are huge and navigable by large ships. Although the cold climate, ice, fog and cliffs are essential elements of the charm of the Great Lakes, they are also dangerous foes for the vessels that must deal with them.

Lake Superior, surrounded by an area whose principal resources are its iron and manganese mines, is situated in Minnesota, adjoining the Canadian border. In the 19th and 20th centuries the ore was transported across the lake by ship. Despite the busy shipping traffic, for many years it was not considered necessary to mark the dangerous craggy shores with a lighthouse.

However, the situation suddenly changed in 1905, following a storm that wrecked 29 ships, all belonging to the same company, touching the hearts and pockets of many people. In 1907 a delegation representing the ship owner damaged by the storm managed to persuade Congress to appropriate $75,000 or the construction of a lighthouse on Split Rock, a 128-foot spur rising above the waters of the northern coast of Lake Superior.

Building commenced in November 1909 and although the task was initially fraught with difficulties – heavy materials had to be transported by boat and then lifted onto the rock by a crane – work proceeded rapidly.

152 ■ The area surrounding Lake Superior, in Minnesota, has many iron and manganese mines. At the beginning of the 20th century, there was a great increase in ore shipping, stimulating the building of lighthouses such as Split Rock.

153 ■ Split Rock is a rocky spur that rises almost 130 feet above the lake. Its strategic position persuaded the United States Congress to appropriate $75,000 in 1907 for the construction of a lighthouse.

The octagonal tower was lit in August 1910, probably by its first keeper, Orren "Pete" Young, who held the post uninterruptedly until 1928.

The octagonal tower is only 52 feet tall, but its position atop a rocky slope means that its light shines out at a height of 180 feet above the lake. The red-brick lighthouse is widest at the base, and tapers toward the summit. The tower is surmounted by a black-painted lantern housing the third-order bivalve Fresnel lenses. These were manufactured by Barbier, Bernard et Turenne of Paris and feature 242 separate prisms, with a range of 22 miles.

Like many other lighthouses, Split Rock was long completely isolated; it was accessible only from the lake. However, modernity eventually reached even this remote spot. In 1915, a sort of cableway replaced the old crane that was used to deliver supplies, but the greatest change came in 1924, with the completion of the nearby highway, which brought the first tourists to the lighthouse by car, to the great astonishment of its keepers. During the 1930s and 1940s, important innovations were made that changed the way in which the lighthouse was run. In 1934 the cableway was dismantled as supplies could now be easily transported by truck, and the foghorn mechanism was equipped with a diesel engine. In 1940 the lighthouse was electrified and the kerosene-vapor lamp was replaced with a 1000-watt bulb. Technological progress also affected shipping, making it increasingly independent. The onboard installation of radars, LORAN systems, and GPS have rendered many lighthouses obsolete and they were conse-

quently deactivated. This was the fate of the Split Rock Lighthouse, which stopped operating in 1969, when it became a historical site.

However, some claim that the lantern of the Split Rock lighthouse was switched off too early, for on November 10, 1975 another terrible tragedy struck these waters. The previous day the *Edmund Fitzgerald*, a freighter bound for Detroit, had left the shore of Lake Superior bordering on Wisconsin carrying over 28,500 tons of ore. The ship ran into the most treacherous storm ever to have hit Lake Superior. Although it tried to avoid the high waves, it listed to one side, lost both its radars, and its deck was — according to a message broadcasted by radio — "washed away by the roughest water it had ever seen." The ship and its crew of 29 men sunk rapidly, without even having had time to lower the lifeboats. Each year since that tragic day the lighthouse has been lit on November 10th to commemorate the loss of the *Edmund Fitzgerald*. This event attracts many people, who thus have the chance of seeing the lantern burning once again.

154 ▪ The tall black lantern on top of the red-brick tower is no longer lit, except on November 10th, during the ceremony commemorating the sinking of the freighter *Edmund Fitzgerald*.

154-155 ▪ The lighthouse's Fresnel lenses, composed of 242 separate prisms, are capable of producing a beam with a range of 22 miles.

LOCATION	COORDINATES	HEIGHT	RANGE	CONSTRUCTION
LAKE SUPERIOR, MINNESOTA, UNITED STATES	47° 14' N 91° 20' W	52 FEET	22 MILES	1910

LA JUMENT

LIGHTHOUSE

[BRITTANY ■ FRANCE]

On January 9, 1904 Charles-Eugène Patron made a will in which he left 400,000 francs for the construction of a lighthouse after having survived a shipwreck. He stipulated two conditions, the first of which was clearly written: "This lighthouse must be built on a rock in one of the most dangerous areas of the Atlantic coast, namely Ouessant Island." The second was that the lighthouse should be completed within seven years, else the donation would be invalidated. Patron died in March of the same year. The Parisian authorities were reluctant to build another lighthouse in the area: the Créac'h Lighthouse already covered that part of the sea and the Ar-Men Lighthouse had just been completed. However, it was decided that another lighthouse in the Fromveur Channel, which leads directly to Brest, would have been useful. The site chosen for its erection was La Jument, where a tragic shipwreck had already occurred

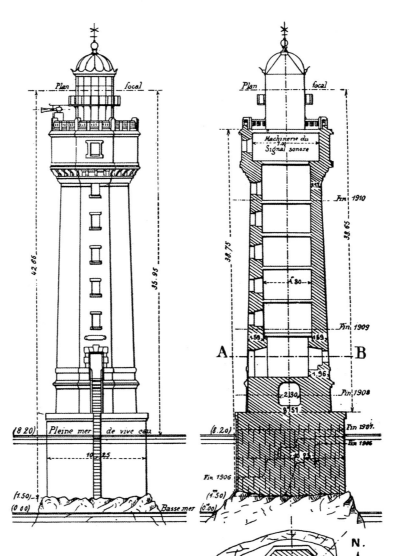

↑

156 ■ The construction plans of La Jument Lighthouse published in *Annales des Ponts et Chaussées* magazine in 1911 show its solid yet still unanchored structure.

157 ■ Several French open-sea lighthouses were built in keeping with the English model. They stand on a rock just a few feet above the water and their bases are often submerged at high tide.

→ →

years earlier, in February 1855. La
Jument is a rocky islet southwest of
Ouessant Island, in an almost inaccessible area with strong currents and
violent sea storms. Sailors have several proverbs about this stretch of
water, one of which says: "Those who
see Ouessant see their blood." Work
commenced in 1904 and difficulties
were immediately encountered. During the first year the terrible conditions allowed the workers to land on
the rock just 17 times, for a total of 52
hours of work. The following year the
sea was even rougher and the men
had to toil in the water, threatened by
the waves. Nonetheless, the strict
organization of the work enabled construction to proceed and the 154-foot
granite lighthouse was inaugurated
on October 5, 1911. Funds were drying
up fast and in their haste to finish the
engineers had not realized that there
was a cavity beneath the rock, that
the islet was not high enough above
the sea and that a nearby reef chan-
neled dangerous waves toward the
base of the lighthouse. The necessary
reinforcement and strengthening
work was carried out in various

stages up until 1940. During the first violent storm the five keepers inside the lighthouse realized that the building was not stable. The waves that arrived from southwest entered the cavity beneath the rock, causing the entire structure to shake dangerously. The glass of the
lantern shattered, water came in through the windows and the mercury spilled out of the
bath in which the lenses floated, poisoning some of the men. This nightmare lasted five days
and nights, until a rescue ship reached the lighthouse. During a subsequent inspection, the engineers realized that the lighthouse was not firmly anchored to the rock and its weight alone
had enabled it to remain standing. The situation was so serious that the Navy evacuated the

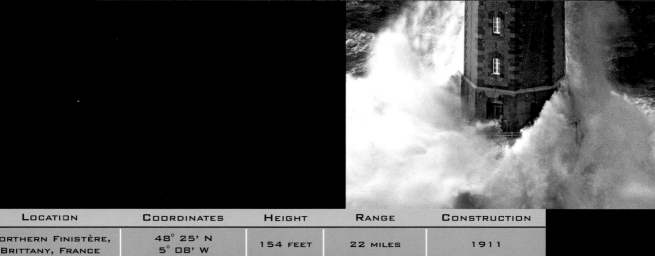

LOCATION	COORDINATES	HEIGHT	RANGE	CONSTRUCTION
NORTHERN FINISTÈRE, BRITTANY, FRANCE	48° 25' N 5° 08' W	154 FEET	22 MILES	1911

158 top and 158-159 ■ This breathtaking sequence illustrates the arrival of a mighty wave that envelops the entire base of the lighthouse. The keeper appears at the door, perhaps unaware of the danger.

159 top ■ The wave has completely submerged the base of the tower, rising in what seems to be an attempt to penetrate the lighthouse. Such situations are not unusual for these lighthouses, fortunately their solid structure enables them to withstand the fury of the sea.

lighthouse in 1918 and the idea of suspending its activity was considered. Nonetheless, it was decided to carry out further reinforcement work, which commenced immediately, with the filling of the cavity beneath the lighthouse. The base was subsequently strengthened with a reinforced concrete jacket. Once again, work proceeded slowly and painfully. The final and most difficult task consisted of anchoring the tower to the rock by means of steel cables, tightened by a traction of 2,755 tons. Charles-Eugène Potron could not have imagined how much the cost of the lighthouse for which he had provided in his will had risen. The keepers subsequently returned to La Jument, and although the lighthouse continued to shake, the glass of the lantern shatter and cracks appear in the walls, nobody heeded these signs any longer. In 1989, the waves completely submerged the lighthouse during a particularly violent storm, but

the tower resisted the onslaught. La Jument Lighthouse is the most exposed and dangerous of all of France's lighthouses. It appears to rise out of the sea, with a hexagonal tower on a terraced base surrounded by a railing and topped with an overhanging balcony that supports a red-painted lantern. The lighthouse was automated in 1991 and is now remotely controlled from Créac'h Lighthouse on Ouessant Island, but its three white flashes continue to illuminate this dangerous stretch of sea every fifteen seconds.

160 ■ The drawing shows a section of the top story and the inside of the lantern room, with the great oval Fresnel lenses.

160-161 ■ The red lantern rests on a sold stone terrace and is surmounted by a handsome cupola, with a sort of polygonal dome on the top.

KÉRÉON
LIGHTHOUSE

[BRITTANY ■ FRANCE]

In comparison with the sober and simple towers of British lighthouses, which all resemble each other very closely, French lighthouses are fairy-tale castles, built using varying forms and methods, in styles ranging from Medieval to Gothic and Art Deco, almost as though their builders drew their inspiration from artistic beauty rather than the practical purposes for which the structures were destined. Kéréon Lighthouse is a good example of this kind of building.

In 1910, the grandniece of a French naval officer, Charles Marie La Dall de Kéréon, guillotined in 1794 during the French Revolution at the age of just 19, donated the sum of 585,000 francs for the construction of a lighthouse named after her ancestor. Many other lighthouses in France were built with private donations because, unlike England, no transit duty was levied on shipping for their maintenance. The running costs were

162 ■ The elegant cupola of Kéréon Lighthouse surmounts a 135-foot solid granite tower. The lantern has a red sector that emits a flash of the same color to signal a dangerous area.

163 ■ Kéréon is one of the most majestic French lighthouses. Its construction was funded by a private donation and it now lights one of the most dangerous areas of sea off the Breton coast.

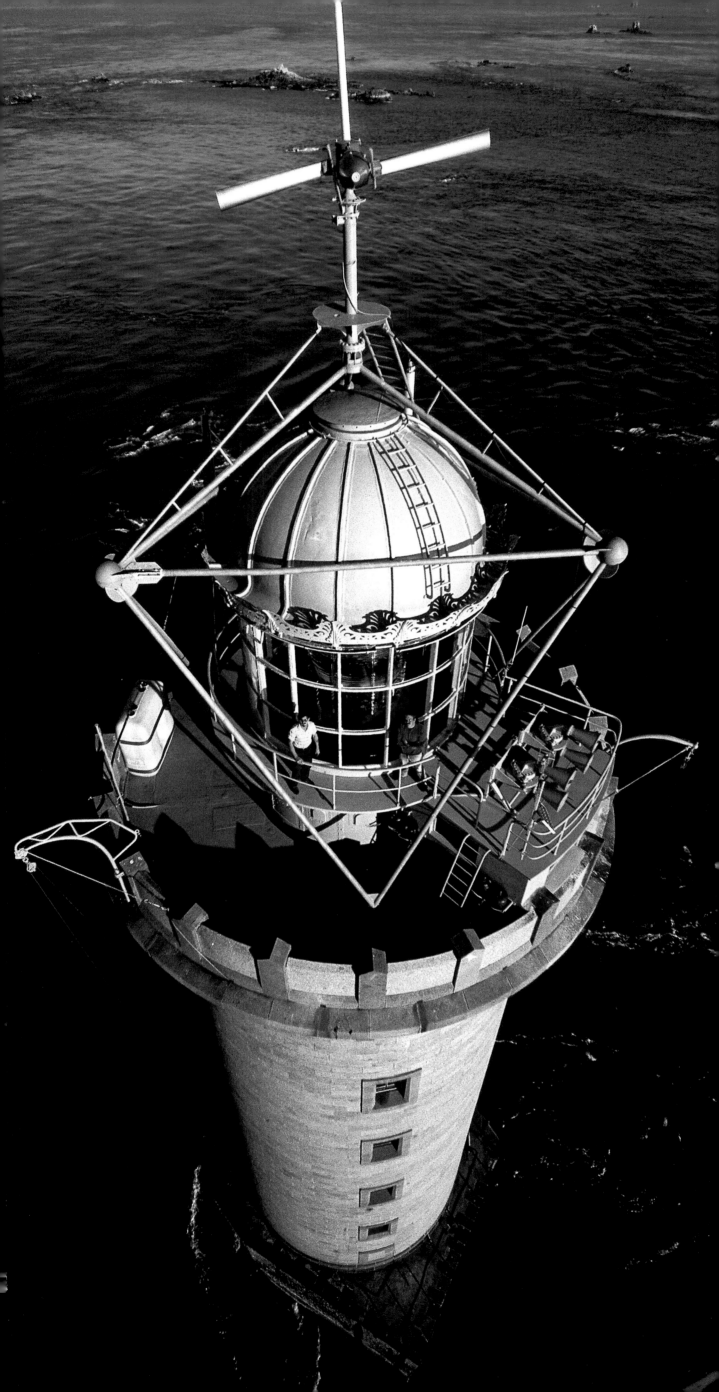

instead covered by the taxes local citizens paid, but extra funds were required to finance the building work.

The tower was erected in the Fromveur Channel, between the islands of Ouessant and Molène, on a little rocky islet called Men-Tensel ("the grim rock" in Breton) off the coast of Brittany. The construction of the building, like that of all open-sea lighthouses, was hindered by various difficulties and completed in terrible conditions. The engineer in charge of the work risked drowning, as did several other men. Nevertheless, despite the outbreak of the First World War in 1914, the 135-foot tower was completed and commenced duty on October 25, 1916. The original kerosene lamp operated until 1972, when the lighthouse was converted to electricity, provided by wind power.

The result was an imposing lighthouse, with a tower resting on a square base often submerged by the sea. Its entire height is dotted with large windows, one above another, while the white painted iron lantern rests on a

round overhanging terrace, supported by stone buttresses and surrounded by a wall. The lighthouse emits a white flash every five seconds, and the rotation of the light comprises a 131° red sector that signals danger at 248° and 190°.

The donation of Charles Marie La Dall de Kéréon's grandniece was so generous that it not only permitted the construction of the lighthouse, but also enabled the creation of unprecedentedly sumptuous interiors. The large entrance hall features a spiral staircase that leads up to a spacious and well-lit kitchen, fol-

164 ■ The rock on which the lighthouse was built has a disturbing name: "Grim Rock." Construction took six years and the men worked in very difficult conditions, as illustrated by these old photographs.

165 ■ French lighthouses were built according to a peculiar architectural criterion. In this case the solidity of the construction has fused with the imagination of the builder to create a medieval-style tower.

Location	Coordinates	Height	Range	Construction
Brittany, France	48° 26' N 5° 01' W	135 feet	White light 19 miles; red light 7 miles	1916

lowed by the roomy keepers' quarters and finally, a huge and very handsome hall of honor on the fourth floor. This round official room is a gem lost in the middle of the sea, with a diameter of almost 20 feet, walls paneled with Hungarian oak, a central sculpted star and an inlaid floor embellished with a large ebony and mahogany wind rose. The hall is dominated by a huge desk at which the keepers used to sit twice a day to compile their daily reports and contact the Lighthouse Service in Brest. The other rooms are also magnificent and decorated with wooden paneling, while the keepers' beds are traditional Breton bunks cut out of the wall, with doors that can be closed to keep out the roar of the wind and the waves. Furnishing the lighthouse was no easy task, as each piece had to be transported by sea and lifted by hoists, but all thoughts of the difficulties that must have been encountered are soon dispelled by the contemplation of this "palace" featuring luxuries that are practically unknown in open-sea lighthouses. The keepers must have been greatly envied by their less fortunate colleagues, except during the changeover, because there is no mooring place for boats on the rock and the transfer was very dangerous for the men, who were lowered down by a cable suspended above a permanently rough sea with strong currents.

Kéréon was France's last inhabited lighthouse. In January 2004 its keepers abandoned it forever, descending by cable as they had always done, to reach the boat that took them away for the last time: automation had triumphed here too. The lighthouse is now remotely controlled by a computerized center in the Créac'h Lighthouse (on Ouessant Island), one of Finistère's 23 signaling towers. The Kéréon Lighthouse has maintained all the beauty and elegance of a historic lighthouse, capable of surviving the most terrible Atlantic storms, and a commemorative plaque fixed to the wall by order of its donor, recalls the last words that the young officer wrote to his father before his execution: "I die an innocent man."

166 and 167 top ■ The interior of Kéréon Lighthouse is entirely wood paneled. Perhaps the elegant paneling made the lives of the keepers more acceptable in a place that obviously entailed daily privations.

166-167 ■ The inside of the lantern room is dominated by the great Fresnel lenses. The perimeter of the cupola is surrounded by an elegant Art-Nouveau style wrought-iron motif.

KÉRÉON
LIGHTHOUSE

168 ■ The keeper descends a cable to reach the waiting boat. This maneuver is performed at each changeover and even the slightest movement of the boat makes it very dangerous.

169 ■ The high base of the tower is often covered by the sea. An exceptional wave hit the lighthouse in 1989, breaking the glass of the lantern and shaking the tower.

PUNTA MADONNA

LIGHTHOUSE

[ISLAND OF PONZA ■ ITALY]

The splendid island of Ponza is situated off the southwest coast of Italy in the Mediterranean Sea, almost halfway between Rome and Naples as the crow flies. The island is an unusual elongated shape and lies on a northeast-southwest axis. Rotonda della Madonna, or Punta Madonna, the site of the lighthouse of the same name, is located on the eastern coast.

This small scrap of land has seen a succession of peoples and civilizations, from the Phoenicians to the Romans, right through to the Bourbons, to whose kingdom the island belonged until the unification of Italy. It was used as a place of detention from 1795 and became part of the Kingdom of Italy in 1861. Finally, in 1928 it was used for the confinement of anti-Fascists.

The old Punta Madonna Lighthouse was built in 1858 and consisted of a five-sided tower topped by a polygonal electric lantern with a range of 15 miles. In the case of power outages, it was replaced by a 6-burner acetylene lamp that the keepers fueled manually. Following the collapse of a cistern in 1954, the entire structure was declared unsound and the resident keepers were sent away. Nonetheless, the lighthouse remained operational and in 1957 the Civil Engineers decided to attempt to consolidate the structure. However, their efforts were unsuccessful and in 1958 work commenced on the construction of a new lighthouse, about 100 feet from the existing one, which was demolished. The new lighthouse became operational on July 20, 1959 and on February 20, 1960 the keepers, or *Fanalisti* as they are called in Italy, moved into the new houses alongside the tower, where they still live today. The cylindrical white tower of the new lighthouse is 26 feet tall, but as it is built on a high rock, it actually rises 200 feet above sea level. Its fixed-light optical system emits three white flashes, followed by a one-second eclipse, and a fourth white flash, followed by an eight-second eclipse, with a range of 25 miles.

171 ■ The breathtaking limestone cliffs of the island of Ponza open like a gash beneath the Rotonda della Madonna Lighthouse, which seems to stand in precarious equilibrium.

Location	Coordinates	Height	Range	Construction
Island of Ponza, Italy	40° 54' N 12° 58' E	26 feet (200 feet above sea level)	25 miles	1858 - 1959

[BIBLIOGRAPHY]

A.A. – *Fari del Mondo* – Edizioni Del Prado 2000

Camillo Manfredini – *Antonio Walter Pescara – Il Libro dei Fari Italiani* - Ed. Mursia 1985

National Geographic Magazine – May 2000

Jean Guichard, Ken Trethewey, – *North Atlantic Lighthouses*, Ed. Flammarion 2002

A. Mitchell – *Historic American Lighthouses* – Ed. Barnes & Noble Books

S. W. Crompton – *The Lighthouse Book* – Ed. Barnes & Nobles Book 1999

R. Christie – D. Hague – *Lighthouses Their Architecture, History and Archaeology* – Gomer Press, Llandysul, Dyfed: 1975

J. Guichard – *North Atlantic Lighthouses* – Flammarion 2002

D. Charles – *Lighthouses of Europe* – Watson-Cuptill 2001

G. Guadalupi e G. Mesturini - *Coral and Desert* – Ed. White Star 2002

A. Terranova – *Skyscrapers* – Ed. White Star 2003

K. Trethewey, M. Forand – *The Lighthouse Encyclopaedia* – Lighthouse Society of Great Britain - 2005 Edition

F. Ross Holland - *Lighthouses* - Metro Books, 2000

James Ward Hyland III - *Lighthouses* - Metro Books, 2000

Michael Vogel - *Lighthouses* - Friedman Fairfax Publishers 2001

[INDEX]

[INDEX]

[INDEX]

[INDEX]

[PHOTO CREDITS]

Page 1 Philip Plisson
Pages 2-3 Yann Arthus-Bertrand/Corbis/Contrasto
Page 4 Paul A. Souders/Corbis/Contrasto
Pages 4-5 Jean Guichard
Page 6 left Jean Guichard
Page 6 right Aaron Horowitz/Corbis/Contrasto
Page 7 Alamy Images
Pages 8-9 Jean Guichard
Pages 16-17 Jean Guichard
Pages 18-19 Marcello Bertinetti/Archivo White Star
Pages 20-21 Philip Plisson
Page 21 Philip Plisson
Page 22 left and right Andreas and Claudia J. Kollner
Page 23 Aisa
Page 24 Antonio Attini/Archivio White Star
Page 25 Richard Cummins/Lonely Planet Images
Page 26 left Antonio Attini/Archivio White Star
Page 26 right Richard Cummins

Pages 26-27 Philip Plisson
Page 27 Richard Cummins
Page 28 Archivio Scala
Page 29 Livio Bourbon/Archivio White Star
Pages 30-31 Marcello Bertinetti/Archivo White Star
Page 31 Stefano Finauri
Page 32 Philip Plisson
Page 33 Philip Plisson
Pages 34-35 Philip Plisson
Page 35 top and bottom Philip Plisson
Pages 36-37 Jean Guichard
Page 38 Alamy Images
Page 39 Alamy Images
Pages 40-41 Alamy Images
Page 41 Alamy Images
Pages 42-43 JW/Masterfile/Sie
Page 44 Photoservice Elekta/Akg
Pages 44-45 Philip Plisson
Pages 46-47 Peter Finger/Corbis/Contrasto
Page 49 Peter Finger/Corbis/Contrasto
Page 50 Philip Plisson

Page 51 Philip Plisson
Pages 52-53 Antonio Attini/Archivio White Star
Page 53 top Giulio Veggi/Archivio White Star
Page 53 bottom Livio Bourbon/Archivio White Star
Page 54 Bernt Hoffmann
Page 55 Kirchner/Laif/Contrasto
Page 56 top by kind permission of Trinity House
Page 56 in centro by kind permission of Trinity House
Page 56 bottom by kind permission of Trinity House
Page 56-57 Kirchner/Laif/Contrasto
Pages 58-59 Philip Plisson
Pages 60-61 Philip Plisson
Page 61 Andreas and Claudia J. Kollner
Pages 62-63 Philip Plisson
Pages 64-65 Philip Plisson
Page 65 Guillaume Plisson
Page 67 Philip Plisson
Pages 68-69 Jean Guichard

[PHOTO CREDITS]

Page 70 Andreas and Claudia J. Kollner

Pages 70-71 Alamy Images

Page 72 Andreas and Claudia J. Kollner

Pages 72-73 Tommaso di Girolamo/ Agefotostock/Contrasto

Page 73 Alamy Images

Page 74 Bob Krist/Corbis/Contrasto

Page 75 Robert Holmes/Corbis/ Contrasto

Pages 76-77 Robert Holmes/ Corbis/Contrasto

Pages 78-79 Philip Plisson

Page 80 Richard Cummins

Page 81 Richard Cummins

Page 82 Richard Cummins

Pages 82-83 Richard Cummins

Page 83 Richard Cummins

Page 84 left and right by kind permission of Trinity House

Page 85 Philip Plisson

Page 86 Andreas and Claudia J. Kollner

Pages 86-87 Philip Plisson

Page 87 Andreas and Claudia J. Kollner

Page 89 Fabio Marino

Page 90 Philip Plisson

Page 91 Guillaume Plisson

Page 92 Philip Plisson

Pages 92-93 Jean Guichard

Page 93 Philip Plisson

Pages 94-95 Philip Plisson

Page 95 Jaques Vapillon

Page 96 Philip Plisson

Pages 96-97 Fernando Alda/Corbis/ Contrasto

Pages 98-99 Guillaume Plisson

Page 101 Mike Dobell/Zefa/Sie

Pages 102-103 Dale Wilson/Zefa/Sie

Page 103 Garry Black/Zefa/Sie

Page 104 Kevin Fleming/Corbis/ Contrasto

Page 105 American Cost Guard

Page 106 left, center and right Bruce Roberts

Page 107 Bruce Roberts

Page 109 Raymond Gehman/ Corbis/Contrasto

Pages 110-111 Bruce Roberts

Page 111 Bruce Roberts

Page 113 Jean Guichard

Page 114 by kind permission of Trinity House

Page 115 Philip Plisson

Page 116 Marcello Bertinetti/ Archivo White Star

Pages 116-117 Marcello Bertinetti/ Archivo White Star

Page 119 Philip Plisson

Page 120 Andreas and Claudia J. Kollner

Pages 120-121 Philip Plisson

Page 122 John Ibbotson

Page 123 Jaques Vapillon

Page 124 John Ibbotson

Pages 124-125 National Archives of Australia; A9568; Macquarie Lightouse - South Head, 1879; 4957034

Page 126 Richard Cummins

Page 127 Ric Ergenbright/ Corbis/Contrasto

Page 128 Angelo Colombo/ Archivio White Star

Pages 128-129 Richard Cummins

Pages 130-131 Craig Tutle/ Corbis/Contrasto

Pages 132-133 Jean-Paul Ferrero/ Auscape

Page 135 Jean Guichard

Page 136 Philip Plisson

Pages 136-137 Guillaume Plisson

Page 137 Jean Guichard

Page 138 Philip Plisson

Page 139 Philip Plisson

Page 140 Philip Plisson

Pages 140-141 Antonio Attini/ Archivio White Star

Page 141 Andreas and Claudia J. Kollner

Pages 142-143 Richard Cummins

Page 143 Alamy Images

Page 144 Barrett & MacKay Photo

Page 145 Kevin Levesque/Lonely Planet Images

Pages 146-147 Barrett & MacKay Photo

Page 149 Jean-Paul Ferrero/ Auscape

Pages 150-151 Jean-Paul Ferrero/ Auscape

Page 151 John Ibbotson

Page 152 Bruce Roberts

Page 153 Layne Kennedy/ Corbis/Contrasto

Page 154 Bruce Roberts

Pages 154-155 Bruce Roberts

Page 156 Collection et cliché Ecole Nationale des ponts et chaussées

Page 157 Guillaume Plisson

Page 158 left and right Jean Guichard

Pages 158-159 Jean Guichard

Page 159 Jean Guichard

Page 160 France/Ministère de l'Equipement-DDE du Finistère- subdivision des Phares et Balises

Pages 160-161 Jean Guichard

Page 162 Philip Plisson

Page 163 Jean Guichard

Page 164 left and right France/ Ministère de l'Equipement-DDE du Finistère-subdivision des Phares et Balises

Page 165 Guillaume Plisson

Page 166 Jean Guichard

Page 166-167 Philip Plisson

Page 167 Philip Plisson

Page 168 Philip Plisson

Page 169 Philip Plisson

Page 171 Philip Plisson

[ACKNOWLEDGEMENTS]

The publisher and author wish to thank the following for their collaboration:
U.S. Coast Guard
Putgarten-Rügen Association
John Ibbotson
Martine Tassel-Leprovost of the Tourist Office
of Le Verdon-sur-Mer
Ninni Ravazza – Chairman of the local tourist office of San Vito Lo Capo (Trapani)
Marco Sebastiano – webmaster www.farodihan.it